Published by
**EN Productions**
P.O. Box 1653, Franklin, TN 37065
www.encountersnetwork.com

# GET eSchool and Other Materials

The following *Getting to Know God and His Word Study Guide* is great for individual study in your own home, with a small group, or in a classroom setting. It also serves as part of the core curriculum for a course by the same title in the **God Encounters Training – eSchool of the Heart**, which also includes a corresponding MP3, CD or DVD class set and other related books. Visit www.GETeSchool.com for more information about this and other life-changing courses.

At the end of each detailed lesson are simple questions for your reflection and review. In a back section of this study guide, you will find the answers to these questions to aid in your learning.

If you have benefited from this study guide, James W. Goll has many other study guides and materials available for purchase. You may place orders for materials from Encounters Network's Resource Center on the website at www.encountersnetwork.com or by calling 1-877-200-1604. For more information, visit the website or send an e-mail to info@encountersnetwork.com.

# Dedication and Acknowledgement

I have had many rich blessings in my walk with the Lord Jesus Christ. Some of these blessings have taken the form of tutors, teachers or equippers the Holy Spirit brought into my life. The most influential of all these human agencies has thus far been the late Derek Prince. His amazing teaching ministry, always centered on the Word of God, radically impacted my life. He scribbled on the wet cement of my life when I was in my twenties. I have never recovered.

With this in mind, I dedicate this *Getting to Know God and His Word Study Guide,* in honor of my grandfather in the faith – Derek Prince.

Thank you Lord, for allowing the teaching influence of this humble, brilliant man of God to cross my path. As another generation arises and now studies these particular notes of mine, as I did Derek Prince's many books and outlines, may concrete be poured into their lives as well. To God be the glory!

**Dr. James W. Goll**
**Encounters Network**

# Table of Contents

# Preface: Getting to Know God and His Word

This *Getting to Know God and His Word Study Guide* comes from my own heart's desire to know my Lord better. Though it is my fifteenth manual, perhaps it should have been my first. These teachings help us with the ABC's. Our goal in life is to know God and to make Him known. I encourage you as you approach this subject of knowing the nature of God, look deeply – not just at the surface level. And, hunger for the things of God, the truth of God, and for God Himself.

The study guide is divided into two sections. The first section is called **To Know Him Is to Love Him**. We'll first look at "God as our Father." What a privilege to be a son or daughter of God. But, if that is the case, then He must be a Father. This section alone could transform your life! Come on a journey and bask in the light of God as Father! Next, we'll look at "Jesus – The Messiah". He is our Master, Savior, Deliverer, and our Messiah! In these lessons you will get a peek at who Christ Jesus really is, and as a result you will love Him all the more. Lastly, we will learn about our personal tutor – "The Person of the Holy Spirit". It takes God to know God, and you can't have enough of the Holy Spirit! We complete this section by getting to know the third person of the Trinity at a deeper level.

The second section is simply called **Knowing God by Knowing His Word**. In it we see the need to lay a firm foundation. We then take time to learn about the origin, effectiveness, and power of God's Word.

In our quest to know our Master, there are many courses to enroll in. Surely being devoted to the study of scripture, a life of worship and prayer, walking in forgiveness, and soaking in His great love are some of the classes we each need to learn from along the way. Let us learn about the nature of God and thus be transformed into His image.

You will find *Reflection Questions* at the end of each lesson and the corresponding answers in the back of the manual. This study guide is prepared to help you know the Lord of Hosts and walk in His nature. Let it be for the glory of God!

**Blessings to You!**

**James W. Goll**

# Section One:

# To Know Him Is to Love Him

# Lesson One:
# God as Our Personal Father

In the beginning of these lessons on *Getting to Know God and His Word*, it is important that we lay a firm foundation. The depth and the strength of the foundation determine what can be built upon it. There is a fixed relationship between the strength of the foundation and the size and permanence of its structure.

Psalms 11:3 states, *"If the foundations are destroyed what can the righteous do?"* This is a question that must be asked and answered sufficiently. Whether you are "investigating the Christian faith," a "new believer in Christ" or have been a "true disciple" for scores of years, it behooves us each to make sure our foundation is solid!

Therefore, I welcome you into this study, where we will learn to become an authentic follower of the Lord Jesus Christ. Let us make sure our foundation is firm.

## I. THE UNFOLDING REVELATION OF GOD

### A. A God Who Can Be Encountered

*"Moses said to God, 'Indeed, when I come to the children of Israel and say to them, 'The God of your fathers has sent me to you,' and they say to me, 'What is His Name?' What shall I say to them?"* (Exodus 3:13)

This question has been asked throughout the ages by all truth seekers. "Who are You?" "What is Your Name?!"

*"And God said to Moses, 'I AM WHO I AM.' And He said, 'Thus shall you say to the children of Israel, I AM has sent me to you.'"* (Exodus 3:14)

Part of the amazing revelation stated here is that God is always "present tense." He is not just the God of the past or "history." He is I AM! In fact, ponder on the thought, "I AM has sent me to you." This is who He is. He is approachable. God is personal. He is now. He is here and wants a living, vibrant relationship with you! He is God who can be and wants to be encountered.

### B. The Many Names of God

Every Name of God reveals another aspect of His nature to mankind. Every new encounter reveals another characteristic of who He really is. Each one of these Names, though, only make up a tiny portion of who God is.

As we bring these many different expressions of who He is together, we see a greater composition of His attributes and greatness.

Consider the following Names of God:
1. Jehovah Jireh – Genesis 22:14 – The Lord Will Provide
2. Jehovah Nissi – Exodus 17:15 – The Lord Is My Banner
3. Jehovah Shalom – Judges 6:24 – The Lord Is Peace
4. Jehovah Tsidkenu – Jeremiah 23:6, 33:16 – The Lord Our Righteousness
5. Jehovah Rapha – Exodus 15:26 – The Lord Our Healer
6. Jehovah Shammah – Ezekiel 48:35 – The Lord Is Present
7. Jehovah Rophe – Psalms 23:1 – The Lord Is Our Shepherd
8. Holy One of Israel – Psalms 71:22
9. The Judge – Genesis – 18:25
10. Eternal God – Deuteronomy 33:27
11. Almighty – Genesis 17:1
12. Fortress – II Samuel 22:2
13. The Lord – Exodus 6:3
14. Living God – Joshua 3:10
15. Lord of Hosts – I Samuel 1:11
16. Lord of Lords – Duet. 10:17
17. Lord of Sabaoth – Romans 9:29, James 5:4
18. Our Strength – Exodus 15:2
19. Most High – Deuteronomy 32:8
20. Father of Lights – James 1:17
(and many more!)

## C.  The Greatest Revelation of All
Perhaps the greatest Name and this revelation of who God is, comes from His inner most being – His heart. Yes, He is our Creator. Yes, He is El Shaddai. But the Lord God Almighty is our Father.

Paul, the bondservant of our Lord Jesus Christ, reveals this to us in his opening remarks in his epistle to the church at Ephesus. *"Grace to you and peace from God our Father and the Lord Jesus Christ."* (II Corinthians 1:2). But this revelation of who God is unfolds even more in Ephesians 3:14, 15. *"For this reason I bow my knees to the Father of the Lord Jesus Christ from whom the whole family in heaven and earth is named."* Ponder it. Reflect. Pause...

God wants a family. God desires fellowship. Therefore, He reveals Himself as our Father.

## II. IN BOTH THE OLD AND THE NEW

### A. From the Old Covenant

1. Deuteronomy 32:6 – Is He not your Father?
2. Psalms 68:5-6
3. Psalms 103:13
4. Isaiah 9:6 – His Name shall be called
5. Isaiah 6:8 – Thou art our Father
6. Malachi 2:10 – One Father

### B. From the New Covenant

1. Matthew 7:11 – How much more?
2. Matthew 23:9 – For One is your Father
3. Luke 11:2 – When you pray say
4. John 1:14 – Begotten of the Father
5. I Corinthians 8:5-6 – One God, the Father
6. Ephesians 4:6 – One God and Father
7. Philippians 2:11 – To the glory
8. Hebrews 12:9 – Father of spirits
9. I Peter 1:17 – Address as Father
10. Revelation 1:6 – Priests to His God

## III. THE PURPOSE OF JESUS

### A. John 14:6-9 – Show Us the Father
Jesus came to reveal God's Fatherhood and Himself as the Way to Him.

*"Jesus said to him, 'I am the way, and the truth, and the life; no one comes to the Father but through Me. If you had known Me, you would have known My Father also; from now on you know Him, and have seen Him.' Philip said to Him, 'Lord, show us the Father, and it is enough for us.' Jesus said to him, 'Have I been so long with you, and yet you have not come to know Me, Philip? He who has seen Me has seen the Father; how can you say, `Show us the Father'"?*

### B. John 14:28 – To Reveal the Greater One
Jesus depicts His relationship as a Son to a Father. He points to another.

*"You heard that I said to you, 'I go away, and I will come to you.' If you loved Me, you would have rejoiced because I go to the Father, for the Father is greater than I."–*

**C.** **John 14:2-3 – To Prepare a Place**

Jesus came to prepare a place for us in the Father's House. Just as Jesus came from the bosom of the Father (John 1:18), so He returns to the Father. But we are now invited to go be where Jesus dwells!

*"In My Father's house are many dwelling places; if it were not so, I would have told you; for I go to prepare a place for you. If I go and prepare a place for you, I will come again and receive you to Myself, that where I am, there you may be also."*

**D.** **John 17:4-6**

Jesus came from a place of glory. He came to reveal the Name of God and glorify God on the earth. Notice the relationship of the Father and the Son portrayed here with deep passion and yearning.

*"I glorified You on the earth, having accomplished the work which You have given Me to do. Now, Father, glorify Me together with Yourself, with the glory which I had with You before the world was. I have manifested Your name to the men whom You gave Me out of the world; they were Yours and You gave them to Me, and they have kept Your word."*

**E.** **John 17:24-26**

Jesus cries out to His Father that His disciples would see His glory. He wants them to partake of His love and to be with Him.

*"Father, I desire that they also, whom You have given Me, be with Me where I am, so that they may see My glory which You have given Me, for You loved Me before the foundation of the world. O righteous Father, although the world has not known You, yet I have known You; and these have known that You sent Me; and I have made Your name known to them, and will make it known, so that the love with which You loved Me may be in them, and I in them."*

## IV. THE PURPOSE OF THE HOLY SPIRIT

**A.** **John 16:13-15 – To Reveal the Son and the Father**

*"But when He, the Spirit of truth, comes, He will guide you into all the truth; for He will not speak on His own initiative, but whatever He hears, He will speak; and He will disclose to you what is to come. He will glorify Me, for He will take of Mine and will disclose it to you. All things that the Father has are Mine; therefore I said that He takes of Mine and will disclose it to you."*

1. The Holy Spirit does not speak on His own initiative.
2. He guides us into truth.
3. He speaks of things yet to come.
4. He glorifies Jesus at all times.
5. He reveals the Father to us.

**B.  Romans 8:14-17 – The Spirit of Adoption**

*"For all who are being led by the Spirit of God, these are sons of God. For you have not received a spirit of slavery leading to fear again, but you have received a spirit of adoption as sons by which we cry out, "Abba! Father!" The Spirit Himself testifies with our spirit that we are children of God."*

1. A mature son or daughter follows the leading of the Holy Spirit.

2. The Spirit of Adoption releases a conviction, a cry, and an awareness within us for our need for the Father.

3. The Holy Spirit confirms to us that we are heirs with Christ and children of God our Father.

## V.  THE AMAZING LOVE OF GOD

**A.  I John 3:1 – Behold, the Love of God**

*See how great a love the Father has bestowed on us, that we would be called children of God; and such we are. For this reason the world does not know us, because it did not know Him.*

**B.  John 3:16 – God So Loved the World**

*"For God so loved the world that He gave His only begotten Son, that whoever believes in Him shall not perish, but have eternal life."*

Compare the following verses:
1. I John 4:9, 18
2. Romans 8:31, 32
3. Romans 8:38, 39

**C.  I John 5:7 – The Three Are One!**

*For there are three that testify.*

## VI. THE FATHER'S BLESSING

### A. The Need We Each Have

There are no perfect individuals on earth. There are no perfect families on earth. There are no perfect fathers. Even the best are a dim mirror of the true eternal Father – God in heaven that loves us! Why is this? My personal thoughts are that we are created to need God! We are created to need a "Father's Love" and a "Father's Blessing" that ultimately only He can fill. There are no grandchildren in the Kingdom of God. The best mentors and examples of the faith should always be used to direct us to another. One who is superior. One who is great. One who is worthy of our worship and praise. We each have the need for our Father's love and blessing.

### B. God Used Human Vessels Representing Himself

In the Book of Genesis, we are given an example where the patriarchal, or Father's, blessing is passed on.

Genesis 49 tells us of Israel's (formerly Jacob) blessing being given to his sons. Each blessing was distinct. Each was individual. Each was a prophetic act. Earlier in Genesis 27 we are shown another picture of the father's blessing being given. This time it was from Isaac to Jacob and Esau. Esau was the firstborn, but Jacob deceived his father and stole the firstborn son's blessing. Once it was given, it could not be revoked!

### C. Today God Uses Imperfect Vessels

Each of us has been created with the need of a Father's love and blessing. For many of us, we have had poor earthly models. Every child born into this world cries out for the love of a father. When received, this impacts acceptance and security. When denied, it leads to rejection. This is the single greatest root cause of emotional and demonic problems in a person's life. Rejection tends to perpetuate itself in a vicious circle from one generation to the next. But this changes through the completed work of the cross of Jesus Christ. Jesus came to introduce us to "Our Father." Through relationship with Him this need and void can be filled. (See other lessons in the study guide *The Healing Anointing* on "God's Remedy for Rejection" and "Healing of the Wounded Spirit" for more on this subject.)

As you seek God's face He will also bring into your life vessels to impart the Father's love to you. Honor is a key that releases this heavenly grace through earthen vessels. Drink from the deep wells of pioneers who have gone before you. Receive His love and acceptance through cracked clay pots in Christ's Name.

**D.   Receive the Father's Love**

1.   Now open your heart and freely receive the love of God the Father through Jesus Christ His Son.

2.   Receive the love of God the Father through a relationship with the Word of God!

3.   Receive the love of God the Father through soaking in the Holy Spirit's presence.

4.   Receive the love of God the Father through reading the lessons of Church history and about leaders who have known the depths of His amazing love.

5.   Receive the love of God the Father by redemptively gleaning glimpses of His shadow through your earthly family members.

6.   Receive the love of God the Father by honoring the anointing of the Holy Spirit upon veterans of the faith. Drink deeply!

7.   Receive the blessing and love of God!

**E.   It Happens by Revelation!**

1.   Read II Kings 1 and 2 where it depicts the life of Elijah and Elisha. Especially note II Kings 2:9-14. Elisha cries out, *"My Father, my Father!"*

2.   The prophet Malachi promises us a last day move of God where the Holy Spirit would restore the *"hearts of fathers to their children and the hearts of the children to their fathers."* (Malachi 4:6)

Let it begin! Let it come forth in fullness! Receive God as Your Father!

# Reflection Questions
## Lesson One: God as Our Personal Father

*Answers can be found in the back of the study guide.*

1. God is not just the God of the _____; He is _____ and wants to be _____.

2. Every _____ of God reveals another aspect of His _____.

3. Jesus came to earth to show us _____ _____.

4. We are created to need a Father's _____ and _____.

5. God uses _____ _____ to represent Himself.

6. Reflect on what your earthly model(s) of a father have shown and have not shown you about God the Father. Write some of these good representations and also misrepresentations of Father God below. Then rate how accurate you feel your perception of God the Father is on a scale of 1 to 10.

*Continued on the next page.*

7. Look at the bullet points in Section IV, D. Pray and ask God which way He wants to reveal the love of God the Father to you in a greater degree. Write down that insight below. If you sense that God wants to reveal Himself to you in another way that is not listed, write that below as well.

8. Choose one of the Names of God listed in Section I, B (Jehovah Jireh, Jehovah Nissi, etc.). Read the Biblical context in which that Name of God was used to reveal a certain part of His character. Then think about one experience in your own life where God revealed a particular part of His character to you. Write below a name that could summarize who God was to you in that situation. (For example, if God showed Himself strong on your behalf during a time of weakness, He would be "God, my Strength.")

# Lesson Two:
# The Amazing Attributes of God

## I. CREATION POINTS TO THE CREATOR

### A. Romans 1:19-20 – Since the Creation of the World
*"For what can be known about God is plain to them, because God has shown it to them. Ever since the creation of the world his invisible nature, namely, his eternal power and deity, has been clearly perceived in the things that have been made. So they are without excuse."*

God's existence and power are clearly seen in the created world in which we live. These things are shown to all mankind and can be known by them, apart from any direct revelation by God through His spoken or written word. The creation points unmistakably to the divine Creator.

### B. Acts 14:17 – God Has Left a Witness
*"Yet he did not leave himself without witness, for he did good and gave you from heaven rains and fruitful seasons, satisfying your hearts with food and gladness."*

God has not left man without any indication of His presence. People who deny the existence of God the Bible labels as "fools" (Psalms 14:1) who suppress the truth, which the creation plainly reveals (Romans 1:18). The created world is evidence for God's existence and power that cannot honestly be denied or ignored. Creation points to its own author, the Almighty God.

## II. THE MANY ATTRIBUTES OF GOD

### A. Genesis 1:26 – Man Created in God's Image
*"Then God said, 'Let us make man in our image, after our likeness; and let them have dominion over the fish of the sea, and over the birds of the air, and over the cattle, and over all the earth, and over every creeping thing that creeps upon the earth.'"*

When God created mankind, He created them in His own image and likeness. Thus, in many respects, man is like God. God is a spirit – He created man as a spirit being. He gave to mankind a free will and a rational mind capable of reason. But there are some attributes that belong to God Almighty and to Him alone.

Genesis 1:1 states, *"In the beginning, God created the heavens and the earth."* In the beginning before anything was there. God existed before anything existed. No one or nothing created God. He has always been (see Colossians 1:17 and Revelation 1:8). God's pre-existence places Him in a position of absolute supremacy. Everything that exists is there because God created it.

Psalms 90:2 says, *"Before the mountains were born*
   *Or You gave birth to the earth and the world,*
   *Even from everlasting to everlasting, You are God"*

There are many created beings in the universe. They all bear, to various degrees, the imprint of their Master. But there is only one Creator and that is God. Thus the qualities, which express God as supreme, are those belonging only to Him! God is all-powerful (omnipotent); He is present everywhere at the same time (omnipresent); He is all knowing (omniscient).

**B.**   **Isaiah 40:25-26 (NKJV)– Omnipotence**
*"To whom then will you compare me that I should be like him?" says the Holy One. "Lift up your eyes on high and see: who created these? He who brings out their host by number, calling them all by name; by the greatness of his might, and because he is strong in power not one is missing."*

God is all-powerful. That is one of His exclusive attributes. God's acts and accomplishments are those that only an omnipotent God could perform. Throughout the scriptures, God is revealed as the "Almighty" (Genesis 17:1, 35:11; Revelation 4:8). God is Almighty because only He is all-powerful.

Since He is omnipotent, there is nothing that is beyond God's ability (Jeremiah 32:17). God's power is more than enough to accomplish His purposes and plans (Isaiah 46:10-11). When God unleashes a measure of His power, it never diminishes His reserve of power. Isaiah 40:28 states, *"the Everlasting God, the Lord, the Creator of the ends of the earth does not become weary or tired."*

While God is all-powerful, He will never use His power to do anything that contradicts that nature. Thus, we find that there are certain things God cannot do. Titus 1:2 tells us that *"God cannot lie."* II Timothy 2:13 states that, *"He cannot deny Himself."* God cannot sin, nor ignore sin in others. His power operates within the confines of His righteousness and loving nature. God is not governed by His power; He always governs that power in keeping with His divine character and nature.

**C.   Jeremiah 23:23-24 – Omnipresence**

*"'Am I a God at hand,' says the LORD, 'and not a God afar off? Can a man hide himself in secret places so that I cannot see him?' says the LORD. 'Do I not fill heaven and earth?' says the LORD."*

God is omnipresent – He is present everywhere at the same time. This does not mean that God and creation are one and the same (Pantheism); God is separate and distinct from His creation. But He is dynamically present everywhere in His own creation.

God's presence fills the universe that He made. Psalms 139:7-12 declares that no matter where David went, the presence of God's Spirit was there. When Solomon dedicated the temple, the "house of the Lord," he proclaimed that God's presence could not be confined to a building (II Chronicles 6:18).

God alone is omnipresent. No man or any angel is present everywhere at the same time. Satan, a fallen angel, is not omnipresent. Nothing escapes God's notice. Even the smallest sparrow does not go unnoticed (Luke 12:6).

No good thing done goes unnoticed by God, and no sin committed goes unobserved by the all-present One. Psalms 94:7-9 says *"And they say, 'The LORD does not see; the God of Jacob does not perceive.'"*

**D.   Isaiah 40:13-14 – Omniscience**

*"Who has directed the Spirit of the LORD, or as his counselor has instructed him? Whom did he consult for his enlightenment, and who taught him the path of justice, and taught him knowledge, and showed him the way of understanding?"*

God's omnipresence points directly to another one of His divine attributes – OMNISCIENCE. To be omniscient means to be "all knowing." Omniscience is intrinsic to God's very nature. God has always known everything there is to know. He sees and knows all that happened in the past, all that is now happening, and all that will occur in the future.

Psalms 147:5 states – *"Great is our Lord, and abundant in strength; His understanding is infinite."* Job 38:4, 18 reinforces this thought. *"Where were you (Job) when I laid the foundation of the earth? Tell Me, if you have understanding. Have you understood the expanse of the earth? Tell Me, if you know all this."* An angel, on the other hand, is finite in his understanding. Man's knowledge comes from an external source. God's knowledge is not externally derived – it is an eternal attribute of His infinite nature.

According to Psalms 139:1-3 – God knows everything about us and is familiar with all our thoughts. Nothing is hidden from Him. If we live uprightly, we can derive comfort from knowing that God is aware of everything we do and even the motivations behind our actions.

God knows us better than we know ourselves. That is why David prayed, *"Search me, O Lord, and know my heart; try me and know my thoughts; and see if there be any hurtful way in me, and lead me in the everlasting way."*

## III. THE MYSTERIOUS THREE IN ONE

### A. The Mystery of the Godhead

The triune nature of the Godhead is one of the most profound mysteries of Christianity. The theological term "trinity" is not found in the scripture though the concept or principle is. The three distinct expressions, or persons, of the Godhead are the Father, the Son (Jesus Christ), and the Holy Spirit. Each of these persons is fully God, none is less God that the other. Yet, these three persons are only one God – not three Gods.

A proper perception of the Trinity is essential. Misunderstanding of this simple and yet complex truth has, in the past, led to error and heresy within the Church. The paradox of how there can be unity and plurality in God at the same time yet be only one God, has been a mystery that has baffled mankind.

These two concepts must be held in balance in order to have a correct view of God. Emphasizing the unity of God at the expense of the plurality of God, will lead to error. By the same token, emphasizing the plurality of God at the expense of His unity will cause the same problem. God is one – Father, Son and Holy Spirit!

### B. Two Paradoxical Concepts

The Trinity of the God-head involves two paradoxical concepts: the unity of God and the distinctions of personhoods within the Godhead.

1. Unity Within the Godhead
   Deuteronomy 6:4 states, *"Hear, O Israel! The Lord our God, the Lord is one!"*

   When God took the children of Israel out of Egypt, He called them away from the polytheism (worship of many gods) of the surrounding nations, telling them that there is only one God in heaven – the God of Abraham, Isaac and Jacob.

Exodus 20:3-7
*"You shall have no other gods before Me. You shall not make for yourself a graven image, or any likeness of anything that is in heaven above, or that is in the earth beneath, or that is in the water under the earth; you shall not bow down to them or serve them; for I the LORD your God am a jealous God, visiting the iniquity of the fathers upon the children to the third and the fourth generation of those who hate Me, but showing steadfast love to thousands of those who love Me and keep My commandments. You shall not take the name of the LORD your God in vain; for the LORD will not hold him guiltless who takes His name in vain."*

A major theme throughout the Old Testament is that there are no gods but God alone (see Isaiah 43:10, 45:5). In John 17:3 God is called the "only true God" because all other gods are false (I Corinthians 8:4) which the scripture labels "lying vanities" (read Jeremiah 10:1-6, 16 for more).

2.  Distinction of Persons Within the Godhead
    *"Let Us make man in Our image, according to Our likeness"* (Genesis 1:26).

    The use of the words "Us" and "Our" in this verse is a reference to the three Persons of the Trinity. These three distinct expressions of God are all portrayed at the baptism of Jesus.

    Luke 3:21-22
    *"Now when all the people were baptized, and when Jesus also had been baptized and was praying, the heaven was opened, and the Holy Spirit descended upon him in bodily form, as a dove, and a voice came from heaven, "Thou art my beloved Son; with thee I am well pleased."*

    Here we see the Son, being empowered by the Holy Spirit, while the Father speaks His approval from heaven. The three Persons of the Trinity (Father, Son, and Holy Spirit) are indeed Persons, and not merely manifestations or modes of God. Jesus the Son, was sent by the Father (I Johns 4:10) and returned to the Father (John 17:13) at whose right hand He is now seated (Mark 16:19). The Spirit who was promised by the Father, was sent by the Son after His ascension. (Acts 2:33; Matthew 28:19; II Corinthians 13:14; John 14:16, 17, 20-23 are similar examples.)

Each of the Persons within the Trinity is fully God. They are not merely manifestations of one God. Manifestations don't converse with one another; neither do they express mutual affection for one another. These are expressions, actions, and activities of persons, not merely manifestations or modes (see John 17:27-28; 17:24).

God is not divided! *For in Him* (Jesus) *all the fullness of Deity dwells in bodily form* (Colossians 2:9). Jesus is no less God than the Father Himself (John 1:1). The scripture also equates the Holy Spirit as being God. When Peter rebuked Ananias, for *lying to the Holy Spirit,* he said, *"You have not lied to men, but to God"* (Acts 5:3-4).

God is one God expressed fully in three persons. Each one is equal to the other. Each one is fully God. Each one possesses all the attributes and characteristics that make up who God is. Yet they are one!

## IV. GOD'S TRUE NATURE

### A. Man's Image of God

Our perception of God's character must be rooted in a revelation of the love of God. Unless a person sees clearly how much God loves him, his concept of God will be twisted and marred by fear. God's intentions toward him will never be clear in his own thinking. Often, we must begin by erasing from our minds some common misunderstandings about God's character. Their distorted views are rooted in the fall of man by sin and used by Satan to paint a dark and twisted picture of God in men's minds.

1. Sin Distorts Man's Image of God
   God created mankind to have fellowship with Him. Sin not only destroyed that fellowship, but also distorted man's image of God. Because of sin, man lost sight of the fact that God is a loving Father. Fear then came in where communion with God had formerly been (Genesis 3:10).

   Sin put God far away from man. He was now wrongly perceived with terror in the minds of those to whom He appeared. Recall the Israelites reaction to the manifestation of God's presence (Exodus 19:18-19). They told Moses to talk to God for them; they would stay in the background at a "safe distance."

2.  Satan Defames God's Character
    Now using man's distorted conception of God to his advantage, the enemy seeks to this day to deceived mankind about God's true nature. II Corinthians 4:4 tells us, *"In whose case the god of this world has blinded the minds of the unbelieving, that they might not see the light of the gospel of the glory of Christ, who is the image of God."*

    The god of this world is Satan. It is he who is boldly and falsely proclaims to mankind that God does not love them. Satan must attempt to keep unbelievers ignorant of the true gospel message and even believers from truly believing, or there would be no question as to whom they would serve. The devil comes with a commonly accepted lie that God is a withholder. But the opposite is the truth. Psalms 84:11 tells us, *"For the Lord is a sun and shield; the Lord gives grace and glory; no good things does He withhold from those who walk uprightly."*

    Believers must settle in their own hearts and minds that God loves them, and is not holding out on them. The fact that God sent His own Son to die for us is eternal, unfading proof that He is a liberal giver and not a withholder (see I Corinthians 1:7; Romans 5:8). *"He who did not spare His own Son, but delivered Him up for us all, how will He not with Him freely give us all things?"* (Romans 8:32)

3.  Religion Affects Man's Thinking
    *"And he sent messengers ahead of him, who went and entered a village of the Samaritans, to make ready for him; but the people would not receive him, because his face was set toward Jerusalem. And when his disciples James and John saw it, they said, "Lord, do you want us to bid fire come down from heaven and consume them?" But he turned and rebuked them. And they went on to another village."* (Luke 9:52-56)

    James and John were ready to call fire down from heaven. They assumed that God reaction to the Samaritan rejection of Christ would be the same as theirs. Jesus' response to them shows that they did not in any way understand the heart of the Father God, nor His reason for sending His Son. James and John projected onto God their own ways of thinking and responding to people.

    Religion (by which we mean – a set of ideas about God formed largely by traditions of men, rather than the Word of God) has done much to promote an incorrect image of God in men's minds. Traditions have portrayed God as being an angry ogre, ready to strike down any offender. He is not perceived as a loving and generous Father. The other side of the coin can be true also. Religious thinking can also produce a God with a wishy-washy kind of love where no values are promoted and everything is fine. I'm okay – you're okay. Both of these religious errors come from not looking properly in the mirror of God's Word.

Isaiah 55:8-9 explains, *"For My thoughts are not your thoughts, neither are your ways My ways, says the LORD. For as the heavens are higher than the earth, so are My ways higher than your ways and My thoughts than your thoughts."*

Never assume that you know what God is thinking unless He tells you through His Word. Presumption always leads to misunderstanding.

### B. God's Image Revealed in His Son
*"He reflects the glory of God and bears the very stamp of his nature, upholding the universe by his word of power. When he had made purification for sins, he sat down at the right hand of the Majesty on high."* (Hebrews 1:3)

Jesus exactly represents God and His great love for man. He is God's statement to the world. "Here I am! Here is what I am like!" In every way Jesus exemplifies the love of God, not only in teaching, but by His compassion, power and lifestyle.

1. By His Teaching
   a) Matthew 6:4, 8-9 – Our Daddy – Father
   b) Matthew 7:7-11 – God gives good things
   c) John 16:26-27 – The Father Himself loves you

2. By His Life
   a) Acts 10:38 – He went about doing good
   b) Matthew 14:14 – He felt compassion
   c) Matthew 15:32-37 – Compassion, power, feeding the hungry

### C. Knowing God's Heart of Love
*"His divine power has granted to us all things that pertain to life and godliness, through the knowledge of Him who called us to His own glory and excellence."* (II Peter 1:3)

We know and walk in the true knowledge of who God is, we then, and only then, can appropriate all things that God has given to us. We must know that He perfectly defines the word love.

1.  By Renewing Our Minds
    a)  Ephesians 3:17-19 – which surpasses knowledge
    b)  Ephesians 2:4-7 His grace and kindness
    c)  Romans 12:2 – be transformed

2.  By Holding Fast Our Confidence
    a)  Hebrews 11:6 – He is a rewarder
    b)  I John 4:16 – Know and believe
    c)  I John 4:18 – Perfect love casts out fear
    d)  Hebrews 3:14

## V.  SUMMARY – THE ALMIGHTY LOVING FATHER

For too long the Church has been paralyzed by distorted views of God. But the Church is awakening to the fact that God is for them and will not hold out on them.

It is this confidence that enabled the early Church to do the mighty works which it did. The Body of Christ will move out in boldness to do the works of Jesus (John 14:12) as we become rooted and grounded in the love of God.

God is supreme. God is powerful. God is all knowing. God is present everywhere. As a loving Father, He is available through His Son Jesus by the power of the Holy Spirit at all times.

# Reflection Questions
## Lesson Two: The Amazing Attributes of God

*Answers can be found in the back of the study guide.*

1. According to Romans 1:20, *Since the creation of the world God's* _____ _____ and _____ _____ *have been* _____ *seen, so all are* *without excuse.*

2. Omnipotent means _____ _____.
   Omnipresent means _____.
   Omniscient means _____ _____.
   God is all of these.

3. A mystery that has baffled mankind is how there can be _____ and _____ in God at the same time yet be only one God.

4. _____ distorts our image of God, _____ defames God's character, and _____ affects our thinking.

5. Reflect on how any of the answers in Question 4 have affected your ability to know the attributes of God. Write down specific instances that God brings to your memory that have hindered your ability to know see God clearly.

*Continued on the next page.*

6.  If someone were to say to me upon observing a distinct characteristic of my son, "Like father, like son," he means that he is not surprised to see my son reflecting one of my personal attributes. John 6:46 says that *no one has ever seen the Father except Jesus.* However, if we know Jesus, we will know the Father (John 8:19; 14:9). Write down ten characteristics that you clearly know about Jesus (i.e. compassionate).

a. _____

b. _____

c. _____

d. _____

e. _____

f. _____

g. _____

h. _____

i. _____

j. _____

Meditate on the fact that what you see in Jesus is what you can expect to find in the Father. "Like Son, like Father." Circle any attribute above where you have not experienced the Father in what you know about the Son. Ask the Holy Spirit to reveal the Father to you in that way.

# Lesson Three:
# Jesus the Messiah Has Come

## I. WHO DO YOU SAY I AM?

### A. Matthew 16:13-14 – Who Do <u>Men</u> Say I Am?

*"When Jesus came into the region of Caesarea Philippi, He asked His disciples, saying, 'Who do men say that I, the Son of Man, am?' So they said, 'Some say John the Baptist, some Elijah, and others Jeremiah or one of the prophets.'"*

1. John the Baptist
   John had already been beheaded and some were saying the Jesus was John brought back from the dead? Why? Perhaps Jesus' prophetic message was like that of John's. Perhaps it was the crowds that had once followed John the Baptist who were now following the Christ. Perhaps it was the miracles or maybe even a guilty conscious of the one replying (Matthew 14:1-12).

2. Elijah the Prophet
   Possibly the listeners remembered the words of the prophet Malachi as written in Malachi 4:5, in which God promised to send the prophet Elijah to earth before the *great and dreadful day of the Lord*. Perhaps again, it was the type of prophetic ministry that Jesus walked in seemed similar to that of Elijah's.

3. Jeremiah the Prophet
   Jeremiah was known as a "weeping prophet." As the new followers of Jesus had observed his life, some of them referred to Him as Jeremiah. Probably this was due to the lifestyle of compassion that He exemplified amongst the people.

### B. Matthew 16: 15-17 – Who Do <u>You</u> Say I Am?

*"He said to them, 'But who do you say that I am?' Simon Peter answered and said, 'You are the Christ, the Son of the living God.' Jesus answered and said to him, 'Blessed are you, Simon Bar-Jonah, for flesh and blood has not revealed this to you, but My Father who is in heaven.'"*

1.   The Most Important Question
     Ultimately, this is the question each man and woman must answer: Who do you say that Jesus is? This is the most important question anyone will be asked in this life. It requires your most significant answer. The answer to this one question will determine each person's present and future destiny.

2.   Jesus Confronts Peter
     Jesus directs his pointed question to Peter. Peter declares that Jesus is the Christ, the Son of the living God. Jesus responds to Peter that his natural senses did not reveal this to him.

3.   Jesus Confronts Each of Us
     It took the "spirit of revelation" for Peter to move from the natural to the supernatural dimension. It is the same for each person. It takes God the Holy Spirit to reveal to us that Jesus is the Son of God!

C.   **Defining Some Terms**
     From Webster's New Collegiate Dictionary:

1.   Messiah – The expected king and deliverer of the Jews; a professed or accepted leader of some hope or cause.
2.   Savior – One that saves from danger or destruction; one who bring salvation; the savior acknowledged by Christians.

Note – The term "Messiah" tends to be used in a Jewish context. The term "savior" tends to be used in a traditional Christian context. It must be realized that the "Jewish Messiah" is the "Christian Savior." Without the Messiah there is no Christianity. Without Judaism there is no Messiah. Without Jesus the Messiah, all mankind is still in darkness.

## II.  JESUS FULFILLED MESSIANIC PROPHECY

There are at least 129 Bible prophecies concerning the first advent of the Messiah – Christ Jesus. Acts 3:24 accurately states, *"Yes, and all the prophets, from Samuel and those who follow, as many as have spoken, have also foretold these days."*

**A.** **Born of a Virgin**
Isaiah 7:14 compared with Luke 1:26-27, 34 and Matthew 1:18, 23, 25.

Isaiah 7:14
*"Therefore the Lord Himself will give you a sign: Behold, the virgin shall conceive and bear a Son, and shall call His name Immanuel."*

Luke 1:26-27
*"Now in the sixth month the angel Gabriel was sent by God to a city of Galilee named Nazareth, to a virgin betrothed to a man whose name was Joseph, of the house of David. The virgin's name was Mary."*

Luke 1:34
*"Then Mary said to the angel, 'How can this be, since I do not know a man?'"*

Matthew 1:18
*"Now the birth of Jesus Christ was as follows: when His mother Mary had been betrothed to Joseph, before they came together she was found to be with child by the Holy Spirit."*

Matthew 1:23
*"Behold, the virgin shall be with child and shall bear a Son, and they shall call His name Immanuel,"* which translated means, *"God with us."*

Matthew 1:25
*"...but kept her a virgin until she gave birth to a Son; and he called His name Jesus."*

**B.** **Born in Bethlehem**
Micah 5:2 compared with Luke 2:1-5 and Matthew 2:5-6.

Micah 5:2
*"But you, Bethlehem Ephrathah,*
*Though you are little among the thousands of Judah,*
*Yet out of you shall come forth to Me*
*The One to be Ruler in Israel,*
*Whose goings forth are from of old,*
*From everlasting."*

Luke 2:1-5
*"And it came to pass in those days that a decree went out from Caesar Augustus that all the world should be registered. This census first took place while Quirinius was governing Syria. So all went to be registered everyone to his own city. Joseph also went up from Galilee, out of the city of Nazareth, into Judea, to the city of David, which is called*

*Bethlehem, because he was of the house and lineage of David, to be registered with Mary, his betrothed wife, who was with child."*

Matthew 2:5-6
So they said to him, "In Bethlehem of Judea, for thus it is written by the prophet:

*"But you, Bethlehem, in the land of Judah,*
*Are not the least among the rulers of Judah;*
*For out of you shall come a Ruler*
*Who will shepherd My people Israel."*

**C.  A Son Shall be Born**
Isaiah 9:6 compared with Matthew 1:21, 25 and Luke 1:31-32; 2:7.

Isaiah 9:6
*"For unto us a Child is born,*
*Unto us a Son is given;*
*And the government will be upon His shoulder.*
*And His name will be called*
*Wonderful, Counselor, Mighty God,*
*Everlasting Father, Prince of Peace."*

Matthew 1:21
*"And she will bring forth a Son, and you shall call His name JESUS, for He will save His people from their sins."*

Matthew 1:25
*"...and (Joseph) did not know her till she had brought forth her firstborn Son. And he called His name JESUS."*

Luke 1:31-32
*"And behold, you will conceive in your womb and bring forth a Son, and shall call His name JESUS."*

Luke 2:7
*"And she brought forth her firstborn Son, and wrapped Him in swaddling clothes, and laid Him in a manger, because there was no room for them in the inn."*

**D.  The Slaughter of Children**
Jeremiah 31:15 compared with Matthew 2:18.

Jeremiah 31:15
*"Thus says the LORD:*
*'A voice was heard in Ramah,*

*Lamentation and bitter weeping,*
*Rachel weeping for her children,*
*Refusing to be comforted for her children,*
*Because they are no more.'"*

Matthew 2:18
*"A voice was heard in Ramah,*
*Lamentation, weeping, and great mourning,*
*Rachel weeping for her children,*
*Refusing to be comforted,*
*Because they are no more."*

## III. THE MESSIAH'S MINISTRY OF TEACHING AND MIRACLES

### A. Blind Eyes Healed
Isaiah 35:5 compared with Mark 10:46, 49-52.

Isaiah 35:5
*"Then the eyes of the blind shall be opened,*
*And the ears of the deaf shall be unstopped."*

Mark 10:46
*"Then they came to Jericho. As Jesus and his disciples, together with a large crowd, were leaving the city, a blind man, Bartimaeus (that is, the Son of Timaeus), was sitting by the roadside begging."*

Mark 10:48-52
*"So Jesus stood still and commanded him to be called. Then they called the blind man, saying to him, "Be of good cheer. Rise, He is calling you." And throwing aside his garment, he rose and came to Jesus. So Jesus answered and said to him, 'What do you want Me to do for you?' The blind man said to Him, 'Rabboni, that I may receive my sight.' Then Jesus said to him, 'Go your way; your faith has made you well.' And immediately he received his sight and followed Jesus on the road."*

### B. Deaf Ears Opened
Isaiah 35:5 compared with Mark 9:17-18, 25-27

Isaiah 35:5
*"Then the eyes of the blind shall be opened,*
*And the ears of the deaf shall be unstopped."*

Mark 9:17-18
*"Then one of the crowd answered and said, 'Teacher, I brought You my son, who has a mute spirit. And wherever he seizes him, he throws him*

*down; he foams at the mouth, gnashes his teeth, and becomes rigid. So
I spoke to Your disciples, that they should cast him out, but they could
not.'"*

Mark 9:25-27
*"When Jesus saw that the people came running together, He rebuked
the unclean spirit, saying to it, 'Deaf and dumb spirit, I command you,
come out of him and enter him no more!' Then the spirit cried out,
convulsed him greatly, and came out of him. And he became as one
dead, so that many said, 'He is dead.' But Jesus took him by the hand
and lifted him up, and he arose."*

### C.    Teaching in Parables
Psalms 78:2 compared with Matthew 13:34-35

Psalms 78:2
*"I will open my mouth in a parable;
I will utter dark sayings of old."*

Matthew 13:34-35
*"All these things Jesus spoke to the multitude in parables; and without
a parable He did not speak to them, that it might be fulfilled which was
spoken by the prophet."*

## IV.    THE MESSIAH PROCLAIMS GOOD NEWS

### A.    Another Would Prepare the Way
Malachi 3:1 and Isaiah 40:3-4 compared with Mark 1:2-4.

Malachi 3:1
*"'Behold, I send My messenger,
And he will prepare the way before Me.
And the Lord, whom you seek,
Will suddenly come to His temple,
Even the Messenger of the covenant,
In whom you delight.
Behold, He is coming,'
Says the LORD of hosts."*

Isaiah 40:3-4
*"He was a voice of one crying in the wilderness:
'Prepare the way of the LORD;
Make straight in the desert
A highway for our God.'
Every valley shall be exalted*

*And every mountain and hill brought low;*
*The crooked places shall be made straight*
*And the rough places smooth."*

Mark 1:2-4
*"As it is written in Isaiah the prophet:*
*'Behold, I send my messenger ahead of you,*
*Who will prepare your way,'*
*The voice of one crying in the wilderness,*
 *'Make ready the way of the Lord,*
*Make His paths straight'*
*John the Baptist appeared in the wilderness preaching a baptism of*
*repentance for the forgiveness of sins."*

## B.  Preach to the Poor

Isaiah 61:1 compared with John 6:10-14 and Luke 4:17-18.

Isaiah 61:1
*"The Spirit of the Lord GOD is upon Me,*
*Because the LORD has anointed Me*
*To preach good tidings to the poor;*
*He has sent Me to heal the brokenhearted,*
*To proclaim liberty to the captives,*
*And the opening of the prison to those who are bound;"*

John 6:10
*"Then Jesus said, 'Make the people sit down.' Now there was much*
*grass in the place. So the men sat down, in number about five*
*thousand. And Jesus took the loaves, and when He had given thanks*
*He distributed them to the disciples, and the disciples to those sitting*
*down; and likewise of the fish, as much as they wanted. So when they*
*were filled, He said to His disciples, 'Gather up the fragments that*
*remain, so that nothing is lost.' Therefore they gathered them up, and*
*filled twelve baskets with the fragments of the five barley loaves which*
*were left over by those who had eaten. Then those men, when they had*
*seen the sign that Jesus did, said, "This is truly the Prophet who is to*
*come into the world."*

Luke 4:17-18
*"And He was handed the book of the prophet Isaiah. And when He had*
*opened the book, He found the place where it was written:"*

*"The Spirit of the LORD is upon Me,*
*Because He has anointed Me*
*To preach the gospel to the poor;*
*He has sent Me to heal the brokenhearted,*

*To proclaim liberty to the captives*
*And recovery of sight to the blind,*
*To set at liberty those who are oppressed."*

C. **Release to the Captives**
Isaiah 61:1 compared with Mark 5:2-4, 9, 15.

Isaiah 61:1
*"The Spirit of the Lord GOD is upon Me,*
*Because the LORD has anointed Me*
*To preach good tidings to the poor;*
*He has sent Me to heal the brokenhearted,*
*To proclaim liberty to the captives,*
*And the opening of the prison to those who are bound."*

Mark 5:2-4
*"And when He had come out of the boat, immediately there met Him out of the tombs a man with an unclean spirit, who had his dwelling among the tombs; and no one could bind him, not even with chains, because he had often been bound with shackles and chains. And the chains had been pulled apart by him, and the shackles broken in pieces; neither could anyone tame him."*

Mark 5:9
*"Then He asked him, "What is your name?" And he answered, saying, 'My name is Legion; for we are many.'"*

Mark 5:15
*"Then they came to Jesus, and saw the one who had been demon-possessed and had the legion, sitting and clothed and in his right mind. And they were afraid."*

D. **Zeal for the Father's House**
Psalms 69:9 compared with John 2:17.

Psalms 69:9
*"Because zeal for Your house has eaten me up,*
*And the reproaches of those who reproach You have fallen on me."*

John 2:17
*"Then His disciples remembered that it was written, 'Zeal for Your house has eaten Me up.'"*

E. **Comes Riding on a Donkey**
Zechariah 9:9 compared with Matthew 21:4-7.

Zechariah 9:9
*"Rejoice greatly, O daughter of Zion!*
*Shout, O daughter of Jerusalem!*
*Behold, your King is coming to you;*
*He is just and having salvation,*
*Lowly and riding on a donkey,*
*A colt, the foal of a donkey."*

Matthew 21:4-7
*"All this was done that it might be fulfilled which was spoken by the prophet, saying:*
*'Tell the daughter of Zion,*
*Behold, your King is coming to you,*
*Lowly, and sitting on a donkey,*
*A colt, the foal of a donkey.'*
*So the disciples went and did as Jesus commanded them. They brought the donkey and the colt, laid their clothes on them, and set Him on them."*

# Reflection Questions
## Lesson Three: Jesus the Messiah Has Come

*Answers can be found in the back of the study guide.*

1. What is the most important question anyone is asked in this life?

2. The Jewish _____ is the Christian _____.

3. Without the _____ there is no Christianity. Without _____ there is no Messiah. Without Jesus the Messiah, the human race is still in _____.

4. There are at least _____ Bible prophecies concerning the first coming of the Messiah.

5. Name five aspects of Jesus' life that were prophesied years before His birth.

   a. _____

   b. _____

   c. _____

   d. _____

   e. _____

*Continued on the next page.*

6. Although the evidence for Jesus' birth, life, death, and resurrection is extensive, some still doubt the historical accuracy of what the Bible records about Him. Examine your own thoughts on this matter. Do you believe that what is recorded in the Bible about Jesus is completely true? Write any questions or doubts you have about the person of Jesus Christ below.

# Lesson Four:
# Wonderful Messiah, Son of God

## I.   THE BETRAYAL OF THE MESSIAH

### A.   By a Close Friend
Psalms 41:9 compared with John 13:21-28.

Psalms 41:9
*"Even my own familiar friend in whom I trusted,*
*Who ate my bread,*
*Has lifted up his heel against me."*

John 13:21-28
*"When Jesus had said these things, He was troubled in spirit, and testified and said, "Most assuredly, I say to you, one of you will betray Me." Then the disciples looked at one another, perplexed about whom He spoke. Now there was leaning on Jesus' bosom one of His disciples, whom Jesus loved. Simon Peter therefore motioned to him to ask who it was of whom He spoke. Then, leaning back on Jesus' breast, he said to Him, 'Lord, who is it?' Jesus answered, 'It is he to whom I shall give a piece of bread when I have dipped it.' And having dipped the bread, He gave it to Judas Iscariot, the son of Simon. Now after the piece of bread, Satan entered him. Then Jesus said to him, 'What you do, do quickly.' But no one at the table knew for what reason He said this to him."*

### B.   For Thirty Pieces of Silver
Zechariah 11:12-13 compared with Matthew 26:14-16.

Zechariah 11:12-13
*"Then I said to them, 'If it is agreeable to you, give me my wages; and if not, refrain.' So they weighed out for my wages thirty pieces of silver. And the LORD said to me, 'Throw it to the potter' that princely price they set on me. So I took the thirty pieces of silver and threw them into the house of the LORD for the potter."*

Matthew 26:14-16
*"Then one of the twelve, called Judas Iscariot, went to the chief priests and said, 'What are you willing to give me if I deliver Him to you?' And they counted out to him thirty pieces of silver. So from that time he sought opportunity to betray Him."*

### C.   Used to Buy a Potter's Field
Zechariah 11:13 compared with Matthew 27:3-8.

Zechariah 11:13
*"And the LORD said to me, 'Throw it to the potter' that princely price they set on me. So I took the thirty pieces of silver and threw them into the house of the LORD for the potter."*

Matthew 27:3-8
*"Then Judas, His betrayer, seeing that He had been condemned, was remorseful and brought back the thirty pieces of silver to the chief priests and elders, saying, 'I have sinned by betraying innocent blood.' And they said, 'What is that to us? You see to it!' Then he threw down the pieces of silver in the temple and departed, and went and hanged himself. But the chief priests took the silver pieces and said, 'It is not lawful to put them into the treasury, because they are the price of blood.' And they consulted together and bought with them the potter's field, to bury strangers in. Therefore that field has been called the Field of Blood to this day."*

## II. THE SUFFERING OF THE MESSIAH

### A. The Messiah Would be Scorned by Crowds
Psalms 22:6-8 compared with Mathew 27:39-42.

Psalms 22:6-8
*"But I am a worm, and no man;*
*A reproach of men, and despised of the people.*
*All those who see Me ridicule Me;*
*They shoot out the lip, they shake the head, saying,*
*'He trusted in the LORD, let Him rescue Him;*
*Let Him deliver Him, since He delights in Him!'"*

Matthew 27:39-42
*"And those who passed by derided him, wagging their heads and saying, 'You who would destroy the temple and build it in three days, save yourself! If you are the Son of God, come down from the cross.' So also the chief priests, with the scribes and elders, mocked him, saying, 'He saved others; he cannot save himself. He is the King of Israel; let him come down now from the cross, and we will believe in him.'"*

### B. The Piercing through of the Messiah
Isaiah 53:5, Zechariah 12:10 and Psalms 22:16 compared with John 19:34, 20:25-27 and Acts 2:23.

(Note: The Romans used the act of crucifixion for only a period of 130 years to execute criminals. It began sixty years before the Messiah was crucified and then lasted only another seventy years as even the Romans judged it as an inhumane way to bring execution.)

Isaiah 53:5
*"But He was wounded for our transgressions,
He was bruised for our iniquities;
The chastisement for our peace was upon Him,
And by His stripes we are healed."*

Zechariah 12:10
*"And I will pour on the house of David and on the inhabitants of Jerusalem the Spirit of grace and supplication; then they will look on Me whom they have pierced; they will mourn for Him as one mourns for his only son, and grieve for Him as one grieves for a firstborn."*

Psalms 22:16
*"For dogs have surrounded Me;
The congregation of the wicked has enclosed Me.
They pierced My hands and My feet."*

John 19:34
*"But one of the soldiers pierced His side with a spear, and immediately blood and water came out."*

John 20:25-27
*"The other disciples therefore said to him, 'We have seen the Lord.' So he said to them, 'Unless I see in His hands the print of the nails, and put my finger into the print of the nails, and put my hand into His side, I will not believe.' And after eight days His disciples were again inside, and Thomas with them. Jesus came, the doors being shut, and stood in the midst, and said, 'Peace to you!' Then He said to Thomas, 'Reach your finger here, and look at My hands; and reach your hand here, and put it into My side. Do not be unbelieving, but believing.'"*

Acts 2:23
*"...Him, being delivered by the determined purpose and foreknowledge of God, you have taken by lawless hands, have crucified, and put to death;"*

C. **None of the Messiah's Bones Would Be Broken**
Exodus 12:46 and Psalms 34:20 compared with John 19:32-33, 35-36 and I Corinthians 5:7.

Exodus 12:46
*"In one house it shall be eaten; you shall not carry any of the flesh outside the house, nor shall you break one of its bones."*

Psalms 34:20
*"He guards all his bones;*
*Not one of them is broken."*

John 19:32-33
*"Then the soldiers came and broke the legs of the first and of the other who was crucified with Him. But when they came to Jesus and saw that He was already dead, they did not break His legs."*

John 19:35-36
*"For these things were done that the Scripture should be fulfilled, 'Not one of His bones shall be broken.'"*

I Corinthians 5:6-7
*"Therefore purge out the old leaven, that you may be a new lump, since you truly are unleavened. For indeed Christ, our Passover, was sacrificed for us."*

**D.   They Divided Up His Garments**
Psalms 22:18 compared with Mathew 27:35.

Psalms 22:18
*"They divide My garments among them,*
*And for My clothing they cast lots."*

Matthew 27:35
*"Then they crucified Him, and divided His garments, casting lots, that it might be fulfilled which were spoken by the prophet: 'They divided My garments among them, And for My clothing they cast lots.'"*

**E.   Marred Beyond the Appearance of Man**
Isaiah 50:6, 52:13-14 and Micah 5:1 compared with Philippians 2:8 and Matthew 27:28-31.

Isaiah 50:6
*"I gave My back to those who struck Me,*
*And My cheeks to those who plucked out the beard;*
*I did not hide My face from shame and spitting."*

Isaiah 52:13-14
*"Behold, My Servant shall deal prudently;*
*He shall be exalted and extolled and be very high.*
*Just as many were astonished at you,*
*So His visage was marred more than any man,*
*And His form more than the sons of men;"*

Micah 5:1
*"Now gather yourself in troops,*
*Daughter of troops;*
*He has laid siege against us;*
*They will strike the judge of Israel with a rod on the cheek."*

Philippians 2:8
*"And being found in appearance as a man, He humbled Himself and became obedient to the point of death, even the death of the cross."*

Matthew 27:28-31
*"And they stripped Him and put a scarlet robe on Him. When they had twisted a crown of thorns, they put it on His head, and a reed in His right hand. And they bowed the knee before Him and mocked Him, saying, 'Hail, King of the Jews!' Then they spat on Him, and took the reed and struck Him on the head. And when they had mocked Him, they took the robe off Him, put His own clothes on Him, and led Him away to be crucified."*

## III. THE DEATH, BURIAL AND RESSURECTION OF THE MESSIAH

### A. His Grave Was Made with the Wicked
Isaiah 53:9 compared with John 19:40-42 and Mark 15:46.

Isaiah 53:9
*"And they made His grave with the wicked*
*But with the rich at His death,*
*Because He had done no violence,*
*Nor was any deceit in His mouth."*

John 19:40-42
*"Then they took the body of Jesus, and bound it in strips of linen with the spices, as the custom of the Jews is to bury. Now in the place where He was crucified there was a garden, and in the garden a new tomb in which no one had yet been laid. So there they laid Jesus, because of the Jews' Preparation Day, for the tomb was nearby."*

Mark 15:46
*"Then he bought fine linen, took Him down, and wrapped Him in the linen. And he laid Him in a tomb which had been hewn out of the rock, and rolled a stone against the door of the tomb."*

### B. Not be Abandoned to Sheol
Psalms 16:9-10 compared with Luke 24:45-47 and Acts 2:29-32.

Psalms 16:9-10
*"Therefore my heart is glad, and my glory rejoices;*
*My flesh also will rest in hope.*
*For You will not leave my soul in Sheol,*
*Nor will You allow Your Holy One to see corruption."*

Luke 24:45-47
*"And He opened their understanding, that they might comprehend the Scriptures. Then He said to them, "Thus it is written, and thus it was necessary for the Christ to suffer and to rise from the dead the third day, and that repentance and remission of sins should be preached in His name to all nations, beginning at Jerusalem."*

Acts 2:29-32
*"Men and brethren, let me speak freely to you of the patriarch David that he is both dead and buried, and his tomb is with us to this day. Therefore, being a prophet, and knowing that God had sworn with an oath to him that of the fruit of his body, according to the flesh, He would raise up the Christ to sit on his throne, he, foreseeing this, spoke concerning the resurrection of the Christ, that His soul was not left in Hades, nor did His flesh see corruption. This Jesus God has raised up, of which we are all witnesses."*

**C.   He Bore the Sins of Many**
Isaiah 53:12 compared with II Corinthians 5:21 and Romans 5:15.

Isaiah 53:12
*"Therefore I will divide Him a portion with the great,*
*And He shall divide the spoil with the strong,*
*Because He poured out His soul unto death,*
*And He was numbered with the transgressors,*
*And He bore the sin of many,*
*And made intercession for the transgressors."*

II Corinthians 5:21
*"For He made Him who knew no sin to be sin for us, that we might become the righteousness of God in Him."*

Romans 5:15
*"But the free gift is not like the offense. For if by the one man's offense many died, much more the grace of God and the gift by the grace of the one Man, Jesus Christ, abounded to many."*

## IV.  A NEW COVENANT FORETOLD

### A.  Sin Enters the World

After God created Adam and Eve, the only commandment that He gave them was they were not to eat of the fruit of the tree of the knowledge of good and evil. If they ate of this tree, they would die (Genesis 2:16-17). Man disobeyed (sinned) and ate from the tree (Genesis 3:6). They were then cast out from the presence of almighty God. (Genesis 3:24)

However, before they were cast out, God made them coats of skins to cover them and their shame (Genesis 3:21). Through the skinning of the animal, blood was shed and death occurred. Here lies the first recorded death of an animal in the Bible. The animal died as a result of their sin.

### B.  The First Covenant – Noah and the Flood

Genesis 8:20-21
*"Then Noah built an altar to the Lord, and took of every clean animal and of every clean bird, and offered burnt offerings on the altar. And the Lord smelled a soothing aroma. Then the Lord said in His heart, "I will never again curse the ground for man's sake, although the imagination of man's heart is evil from his youth; nor will I again destroy every living thing as I have done."*

Genesis 9:11, 13-15
*"Thus I establish My covenant with you: Never again shall all flesh be cut off by the waters of the flood; never again shall there be a flood to destroy the earth. I set My rainbow in the cloud, and it shall be for the sign of the covenant between Me and the earth. It shall be, when I bring a cloud over the earth, that the rainbow shall be seen in the cloud."*

### C.  The Abrahamic Covenant – The Second Covenant

Genesis 12:3
*"I will bless those who bless you,
And I will curse him who curses you;
And in you all the families of the earth shall be blessed."*

Genesis 17:7-10
*"And I will establish My covenant between Me and you and your descendants after you in their generations, for an everlasting covenant, to be God to you and your descendants after you. Also I give to you and your descendants after you the land in which you are a stranger, all the land of Canaan, as an everlasting possession; and I will be their God. And God said to Abraham: "As for you, you shall keep My covenant, you and your descendants after you throughout their generations. This is My covenant which you shall keep, between Me and you and your descendants after you: every male child among you shall be circumcised."*

### D. The Covenant at Sinai – The Third Covenant

Deuteronomy 5:2-3
*"The Lord our God made a covenant with us in Horeb. The Lord did not make this covenant with our fathers, but with us, those who are here today, all of us who are alive."*

Exodus 24:5-8
*"Then he sent young men of the children of Israel, who offered burnt offerings and sacrificed peace offerings of oxen to the Lord. And Moses took half the blood and put it in basins, and half the blood he sprinkled on the altar. Then he took the Book of the Covenant and read in the hearing of the people. And they said 'All that the Lord has said we will do, and be obedient.'"*

### E. The New Covenant – The Messiah Fulfills

Jeremiah 31:31-34
*"Behold, the days are coming, says the Lord, when I will make a new covenant with the house of Israel and with the house of Judah. Not according to the covenant that I made with their fathers in the day that I took them by the hand to lead them out of the land of Egypt, My covenant which they broke, though I was a husband to them, says the Lord. But this is the covenant that I will make with the house of Israel after those days, says the Lord: I will put My law in their minds, and write it on their hearts; and I will be their God, and they shall be My people. No more shall every man teach his neighbor, and every man his brother, saying, 'Know the Lord,' for they all shall know Me, from the least of them to the greatest of them, says the Lord. For I will forgive their iniquity, and their sin I will remember no more."*

Isaiah 42:9
*"Behold, the former things have come to pass, and new things I declare; before they spring forth I tell you of them."*

The Hebrew word for New Covenant is "chadesh." It is defined as "fresh," "new thing." It is used only 48 times in the scriptures. This word is used in Isaiah 42:9.

Ezekiel 36:25-27
*"Then I will sprinkle clean water on you, and you shall be clean; I will cleanse you from all your filthiness and from all your idols. I will give you a new heart and put a new spirit within you; I will take the heart of stone out of your flesh and give you a heart of flesh. I will put My Spirit within you and cause you to walk in My statutes, and you will keep My judgments and do them."*

Ezekiel 11:19-20
*"Then I will give them one heart, and I will put a new spirit within them, and take the stony heart out of their flesh, and give them a heart of flesh, that they may walk in My statutes and keep My judgments and do them; and they shall be My people, and I will be their God."*

II Corinthians 5:19, 21
*"That is, that God was in Christ reconciling the world to Himself, not imputing their trespasses to them, and has committed to us the word of reconciliation. For He made Him who knew no sin to be sin for us, that we might become the righteousness of God in Him."*

Colossians 1:20-22
*"And by Him to reconcile all things to Himself, by Him, whether things on earth or things in heaven, having made peace through the blood of His cross. And you, who once were alienated and enemies in your mind by wicked works, yet now He has reconciled in the body of His flesh through death, to present you holy, and blameless, and above reproach in His sight."*

Hebrews 13:20-21
*"Now may the God of peace who brought up our Lord Jesus from the dead, that great Shepherd of the sheep, through the blood of the everlasting covenant, make you complete in every good work to do His will, working in you what is well pleasing in His sight, through Jesus Christ, to whom be glory forever and ever. Amen."*

## V.   JESUS CHRIST – THE KING MESSIAH

### A.   A Promise to King David

II Samuel 7:12-16
*"When your days are fulfilled and you rest with your fathers, I will set up your seed after you, who will come from your body, and I will establish his kingdom. He shall build a house for My name, and I will establish the throne of his kingdom forever. I will be His Father, and he shall be My son. If he commits iniquity, I will chasten him with the rod of men and with the blows of the sons of men. But My mercy shall not depart from him, as I took it from Saul, whom I removed from before you. And your house and your kingdom shall be established forever before you. Your throne shall be established forever."*

Psalms 89:34-36
*"My covenant I will not break,*
*Nor alter the word that has gone out of My lips.*
*Once I have sworn by My holiness;*
*I will not lie to David:*
*His seed shall endure forever,*
*And his throne as the sun before Me;"*

Isaiah 7:13-14
*"Then he said, 'Hear now, O house of David! Is it a small thing for you to weary men, but will you weary my God also? Therefore the Lord Himself will give you a sign: Behold, the virgin shall conceive and bear a Son, and shall call His name Immanuel.'"*

Mark 10:46-48
*"Then they came to Jericho. As He went out of Jericho with His disciples and a great multitude, blind Bartimaeus, the son of Timaeus, sat by the road begging. And when he heard that it was Jesus of Nazareth, he began to cry out and say, 'Jesus, Son of David, have mercy on me!' Then many warned him to be quiet; but he cried out all the more, "Son of David, have mercy on me!"*

### B.   King Messiah Is Not a Mere Man

Daniel 7:9-10
*"I watched till thrones were put in place, and the Ancient of Days was seated; His garment was white as snow, and the hair of His head was like pure wool. His throne was a fiery flame. Its wheels a burning fire; a fiery stream issued and came forth from before Him. A thousand thousands ministered to Him; ten thousand times then thousand stood before Him. The court was seated. And the books were opened."*

Psalms 2:6-10

*"Yet I have set My King on My holy hill of Zion. I will declare the decree: The Lord has said to me, 'You are My son, today I have begotten you. Ask of Me, and I will give you the nations for your inheritance, and the ends of the earth for your possession. You shall break them with a rod of iron; you shall dash them to pieces like a potter's vessel. Now therefore, be wise, O kings; be instructed, you judges of the earth.'"*

Daniel 7:13-14

*"I was watching in the night visions, and behold, one like the son of man, coming with the clouds of heaven! He came to the Ancient of Days, and they brought Him hear before Him. Then to Him was given dominion and glory and a kingdom that all peoples, nations, and languages should serve Him. His dominion is an everlasting dominion, which shall not pass away, and His kingdom the one which shall not be destroyed."*

## C.   Jesus Christ Is the King Messiah

Matthew 1:1, 6-7; 11-13
Matthew 1:18, 20-23
Matthew 26:63-65
Revelation 19:11-16

# Reflection Questions
## Lesson Four: The Wonderful Messiah, Son of God

*Answers can be found in the back of the study guide.*

1. The Romans used the act of crucifixion for only a period of _____ years to execute criminals.

2. Death by crucifixion began _____ years before the Messiah was crucified and then lasted only another _____ years.

3. What does this short time frame tell you about the fulfillment of Old Testament prophecy?

4. Name five additional aspects of Jesus' life that were prophesied years before His birth.

    a. _____

    b. _____

    c. _____

    d. _____

    e. _____

*Continued on the next page.*

5. Before moving on further in this study, research any questions or doubts you wrote out in Number 6 of Lesson Nine's *Reflection Questions*. Write out your conclusions. I especially recommend reading applicable sections of *Evidence That Demands a Verdict* by Josh McDowell (see the Resource Recommendation Page in the back of this manual for more information).

6. What is the first instance in human history of death and the shedding of blood?

8. The word covenant means "an eternal agreement cut with blood." How does this definition manifest in God's covenant with Moses?

10. Read Daniel 7:9-10, 13-14 and Revelation 19:11-16. Compare below His first coming and life on earth to His second coming and reign on the earth – the ultimate fulfillment of all Messianic prophecy.

# Lesson Five:
# The Person of the Holy Spirit

## I. THE THIRD PERSON OF THE GODHEAD

John 16:13-15
*"However, when He, the Spirit of truth, has come, He will guide you into all truth; for He will not speak on His own authority, but whatever He hears He will speak; and He will tell you things to come. He will glorify Me, for He will take of what is mine and declare it to you. All things that the Father has are mine. Therefore I said that He will take of mine and declare it to you."*

Acts 1:8
*"But you shall receive power when the Holy Spirit has come upon you."*

### A. The Most Overlooked Person of the Godhead

1. Of the eternal Godhead, which we have studied – God the Father, Jesus Christ the Son, and the Holy Spirit – The Holy Spirit seems to be the most misunderstood and least appreciated. Yet the Holy Spirit is the most vital and intimate aspect of our personal conversion, growth in Christ and the ongoing building of God's glorious Kingdom on the earth.

2. Andrew Murray states: "The Father is the eternal being – I AM – the hidden foundation of all things and fountain of all life. The Son is the outward form, express image, the revelation of God. The Spirit is the executive power of the Godhead. The nature of the hidden unity is revealed and made known in the Son, and is imparted to us and is experienced by us through the agency of the Spirit." [1]

3. Part of this misunderstanding comes from the fact that His work is NEVER to call attention to Himself but only to exalt the Lord Jesus. (John 16:14)

### B. The Primary Purpose

1. Our purpose in this session is to bring us into deeper understanding and deeper intimacy with the person of the Holy Spirit, and through this union experience greater power, greater joy and greater hope.

2. The Holy Spirit is the third divine Person of the eternal Godhead, co-equal, co-eternal, and co-existent with the Father and the Son. It is His ministry to convict and convert man as well as to reveal the Son and the Father to the believer. Since the glorification of the Lord Jesus Christ, the Holy Spirit in all His glorious operation is working through all who believe on the Father through the Son. This is why the present era is known as the age of the Holy Spirit. [2]

## II. THE HOLY SPIRIT IS A PERSON

The Spirit is more than a mere influence as some suggest. He is a real Person with a mind, feelings and will just like the Father and the Son.

A. **The Holy Spirit was sent by the Father to take the place of Jesus in the earth.** Jesus said, *"It is to your advantage that I go away..."* (John 16:7-15)

A. **The promise, *"He will guide you...whatever He hears...He will speak...He shall glorify Me..."*** (John 16:13-14)

B. **He speaks to Philip.** (Acts 8:29)

C. **He strives.** (Genesis 6:3)

D. **He can be lied against.** (Acts 5:3)

E. **He can be grieved.** (Ephesians 4:30)

F. **He can be sinned against.** (Mark 3:29)

G. **He searches all things.** (I Corinthians 2:10-11)

H. **He makes intercession for us.** (Romans 8:26)

I. **He distributes gifts.** (I Corinthians 2:11)

J. **He is called the Counselor.** (John 15:26)

K. **He is called the Comforter or Helper.** (John 14:26)

## III. THE DEITY OF THE HOLY SPIRIT

"The personality and deity of the Holy Spirit are practical teachings, for it is by the activity of this divine being that the gospel of salvation in Jesus Christ is made clear to us and changes our lives. He is the key to a vital and truly personal religion." [3] (quote from James Montgomery Boice)

**A.  He is specifically called God.** (Acts 5:4; II Corinthians 3:17)

**B.  "Do you not know that you are a temple of God and that the Spirit of God dwells in you?"** (I Corinthians 3:16)

**C.  He is eternal.** (Hebrew 9:14)

**D.  He is omnipresent.** (Psalms 139:7)

**E.  He is the Spirit of Life.** (Romans 8:2)

**F.  He is the Spirit of Truth.** (John 16:13)

**G.  The Spirit participated in creation.** (Genesis 1:2)

**H.  He participates in regeneration.** (John 3:8)

**I.  Jesus was raised from the dead by the Spirit.** (Romans 8:11)

## IV. THE FIVE GREAT REDEMPTIVE ACTS

When it comes to blessing the human race, no Person of the Godhead is willing to be left out. In each of the five great interventions of God in redemption, each person of the Godhead is directly involved.

**A.  The Incarnation of Jesus**
God the Father by the agency of the Holy Spirit incarnated Jesus the Son in the womb of the Virgin Mary (Luke 1:35; Matthew 1:20).

**B.  The Earthly Ministry of Jesus**
God the Father anointed Jesus the Son with the power of the Holy Spirit. The result: healing and deliverance for humanity.

Acts 10:38
*"You know of Jesus of Nazareth, how God anointed Him with the Holy Spirit and with power, and how He went about doing good and healing all who were oppressed by the devil, for God was with Him."*

**C.** **The Atonement of Jesus**

Jesus the Son offered himself to God the Father through the Holy Spirit.

Hebrews 9:14
*"How much more shall the blood of Christ, who through the eternal Spirit offered Himself without spot to God, cleanse your conscience from dead works to serve the living God?"*

**D.** **The Resurrection of Jesus**

God the Father raised up Jesus the Son by the power of the Holy Spirit

Romans 1:4
*"...who was declared the Son of God with power by the resurrection from the dead, according to the Spirit of holiness."*

Romans 6:4
*"Therefore we have been buried with Him through baptism into death, so that as Christ was raised from the dead through the glory of God the Father, so we too might walk in newness of life."*

**E.** **The Gift of the Holy Spirit**

At Pentecost Jesus the Son received from God the Father the gifts of the Holy Spirit and poured them out upon His disciples (Acts 2:32-33). Likewise, the ongoing relationship of God to his people in this age directly involves all three personas of the Godhead. The end purpose of God is that we come to Him as Father; but we have access to God the Father only through Jesus the Son by the Holy Spirit (Ephesians 2:18-19). Similarly, God the Father indwells His people only in Jesus the Son through the Holy Spirit (Ephesians 2:22).

Ephesians 2:22
*"In whom you also are being built together into a dwelling place of God in the Spirit."*

## V. THE CONTINUING ACTIVITY OF THE HOLY SPIRIT

**A.** **Another Would Come After Him**

Toward the close of His earthly ministry Jesus prepared His disciples for the fact that, as a person, He would leave them and that another persona – the Holy Spirit – would then come to take His place. He emphasized the following truths:

1.   The Holy Spirit is the promise of the Father.

Luke 24:45-49
*"Then He said to them, 'Thus it is written, and thus it was necessary for the Christ to suffer and to rise from the dead the third day, and that repentance and remission of sins should be preached in His name to all nations, beginning at Jerusalem. And you are witnesses of these things. Behold, I send the promise of my Father upon you; but tarry in the city of Jerusalem until you are endued with power from on high.'"*

Acts 1:4
*"And being assembled together with them, He commanded them not to depart from Jerusalem, but to wait for the Promise of the Father, "which," He said, "you have heard from Me.""*

2.   There was to be an exchange of Persons. First, Jesus was to leave; then, the Holy Spirit would come in His place.

John 14:15-18
*"If you love Me, keep My commandments. And I will pray the Father, and He will give you another Helper, that He may abide with you forever – the Spirit of truth, whom the world cannot receive, because it neither sees Him nor knows Him; but you know Him, for He dwells with you and will be in you. I will not leave you orphans; I will come to you."*

## B.   The Main Purposes of the Holy Spirit

John 14:18 refers to the coming of Jesus, at Pentecost, in the Person of the Holy Spirit. John 14:3 refers to the Second Coming of Jesus, in His own Person, at the close of the age. Three main purposes for which the Holy Spirit came:

1.   To complete the ministry of Christ (John 14:25; 16:12-13).
2.   To form the corporate Body of Christ.
3.   To prepare the Bride of Christ.

## C.   The Now-Presence Representative of the Godhead

In this age, the Holy Spirit is the resident, personal representative of the Godhead on earth. His dwelling place is described in two ways:

1.   I Cor. 3:16-17 refers to the collective temple – the Church.

2.   I Cor. 6:19-20 refers to the individual temple – the physical body of each believer. Jesus is Lord over the Church; the Holy Spirit is Lord in the Church.

## D.    From the Resurrection Onward

1.    From resurrection onward, Jesus operated always and only through the Holy Spirit.

    Romans 6:4
    *"Therefore we were buried with Him through baptism into death, that just as Christ was raised from the dead by the glory of the Father, even so we also should walk in newness of life."*

    Romans 8:10-11
    *"But if the Spirit of Him who raised Jesus from the dead dwells in you, He who raised Christ from the dead will also give life to your mortal bodies through His Spirit who dwells in you."*

    Acts 1:2
    *"Until the day in which He was taken up, after He through the Holy Spirit had given commandments to the apostles whom He had chosen."*

2.    We need to be equally dependent upon the Holy Spirit for Christian living.

    Romans 8:14-15
    *"For as many as are led by the Spirit of God, these are sons of God. For you did not receive the spirit of bondage again to fear, but you received the Spirit of adoption by whom we cry out, 'Abba, Father.'"*

    Galatians 3:1
    *"O, foolish Galatians! Who has bewitched you that you should not obey the truth, before whose eyes Jesus Christ was clearly portrayed among you as crucified?"*

    Galatians 5:3-4
    *"You have become estranged from Christ, you who attempt to be justified by law; you have fallen from grace."*

3.    At the end of the age the person of the Holy Spirit works with the bride. Together we cry out, "Come, Lord Jesus!"

    Revelations 1:17
    *"And when I saw Him, I fell at His feet as dead. But He laid His right hand on me, saying to me, "Do not be afraid; I am the First and the Last."*

# Reflection Questions
## Lesson Five: The Person of the Holy Spirit

*Answers can be found in the back of the study guide.*

1. The Holy Spirit is the most vital and intimate aspect of our _____ _____, _____ _____ _____, and the ongoing building of _____ _____ on earth.

2. More than a mere influence as some suggest, the Holy Spirit is the third divine Person of the eternal Godhead, _____, _____, and _____ with the Father and the Son.

3. Name the five great redemptive acts in which each Person of the Godhead were directly involved.

   a. _____

   b. _____

   c. _____

   d. _____

   e. _____

4. The Holy Spirit came to...

   a. _____

   b. _____

   c. _____

*Continued on the next page.*

5. The Holy Spirit resides collectively in the _____, and individually in the physical body of each _____.

6. From the resurrection onward, Jesus operated _____ and _____ through the Holy Spirit.

7. Meditate on Romans 6:4 and Romans 8:10-11. Contemplate that "the glory of the Father" that raised Christ Jesus from the dead is the same Person who empowers us to "walk in newness of life." Below list the ways that the Holy Spirit is empowering you right now to walk in newness of life.

8. List below characteristics of Jesus' life and ministry that stand out to you. Then listen to the Holy Spirit and write down what He desires to be the primary characteristics of your life and ministry in the coming days, months, and years. Bring these things regularly before the Lord in prayer until you are walking fully in the power of the Holy Spirit.

| **THE LIFE OF CHRIST** | **MY LIFE** |
| Empowered by the Holy Spirit | Empowered by the Holy Spirit |
| | |

# Lesson Six:
# Holy Spirit, You Are Welcome Here!

"The Holy Spirit has personality, though not a corporate body. Personality is that which possesses intelligence, feeling, and will. When one possesses the characteristics, properties **and** qualities of personality, then personality can be attributed to that being. Personality, when used in reference to divine beings, cannot be measured by human standards."

by Dick Iverson from *The Holy Spirit Today* [4]

## I. THE ACTIVITIES OF THE DOVE OF GOD

As we look at the work and activity and the Holy Spirit – the Dove of God, we will derive help as we consider the names and symbols used in scripture. Let's remember, this is all about knowing God better – more intimately. We want to know the Holy Spirit and welcome more of His presence in our lives both individually and in every sphere of life ministry. We want the Dove of God to "descend upon" us but to dwell with us, stay with us. We want to be a "perch" where the Dove of God will come and sit and remain!

Now names are extremely significant. They help give meaning, definition, identity and purpose to a person, city, and a nation and even to God Himself. As seen in previous teachings, the Father and the Son have distinct names ascribed to them illustrating for us part of their nature, characteristics, function, purpose and ministry.

The following is not a comprehensive list, but it does give us a glimpse into the major names in scripture of the Third Person of the Godhead.

### A. The Titles of the Holy Spirit
1. The Spirit of God – Genesis 1:2
2. The Holy Spirit – Luke 11:13
3. The Spirit of Grace – Hebrews 10:29
4. The Spirit of Burning – Isaiah 4:4
5. The Spirit of Truth – John 14:17, 16:13
6. The Spirit of Life – Romans 8:2
7. The Spirit of Wisdom and Revelation – Ephesians 1:17; Isaiah 11:2, 61:1-2
8. The Spirit of Promise – Ephesians 1:3; Joel 2:28; Ezekiel 36:27; Luke 24:49; Acts 1:4; Galatians 3:14

9. The Spirit of Glorify – I Peter 4:14
10. The Spirit of Christ – I Corinthians 3:16; Romans 8:9
11. The Comforter – John 14:16
12. The Spirit of Adoption – Romans 8:15

**B. The Symbols of the Holy Spirit**

Symbols are often used in scripture to assist us in our understanding concerning various aspects or characteristics of a given subject, in this case the Holy Spirit Himself. Not all symbols are used as official names or titles, though they are often tools to bring to grant us more understanding.

1. As Fire – Isaiah 4:4; Matthew 3:11
   The primary emphasis of fire in the Scriptures relates to the act of purging, sanctifying, purifying, and burning out the dross etc. Let His fire come!

2. As Wind – Ezekiel 37:7-10; John 3:8; Acts 2:2-3
   We cannot see the wind but we can feel the wind, hear the wind, see the effects of the wind and channel the wind into useful purposes. So is our relationship with the Wind of the Holy Spirit. He comes to powerfully propel us into forward motion.

3. As Water – John 7:38-39; 1 John 4:14; I Cor. 10:1-3; Titus 3:5
   Water satisfies our thirst. It is one thing we need every day to live. Water also cleanses and washes away the filth or defilement of the day. It refreshes us and brings into the flow of the true Spiritual life.

4. As a Seal – Ephesians 1:13-14
   The precious Holy Spirit is given to us as a pledge or earnest down payment of the fullness of that which is yet to come. The revelation of the seal establishes the fact we are His forever.

5. As Oil – Psalms 89:20, 92:10; Acts 10:38; 1 John 2:27; Matthew 25:3
   Oil in the Old Testament was used for used for the consecrating and anointing of Kings, Priests and Prophets. It represented that you were chosen by God and divinely empowered for service. No one dared enter into any of these functions or roles without the oil. In the New Testament, and of course today, the oil of the Holy Spirit speaks of healing, the soothing comfort, illumination and strengthening of the God. Send us the oil Lord!

6. As the Dove – Matthew 3:16
The dove nature of the Holy Spirit is a beautiful truth indeed. It displays for us the gentleness, tenderness, innocence, sensitivity, purity and peace of God.

Oh how I love the Dove of God! I want to be sensitive to His cooing and wooing. I want Him to come and sit on my shoulder and never go away. Come Holy Spirit and make your dwelling place among your people, the church of the living God once again!

## II. THE HOLY SPIRIT'S RELATIONSHIP TO THE BELIEVER

In one sense, it is actually the Holy Spirit that we first meet in our relationship with God. He is the one who makes Jesus into a living reality instead of just a great historical figure. He is the one who convicts us of sin, righteousness and judgment to come.

**A. Regenerates - The New Birth**
Titus 3:5; John 3:3; I Corinthians 12:13

**B. Indwells of the Believer**
John 14:17; Romans 8:9; 2 Timothy 1:14

**C. Sets the Believer Free!**
Romans 8:1-2; Ephesians 1:19, 3:16; Romans 12:1-2; also I Corinthians 3:18, 4:16; Colossians 3:10; Ephesians 4:23

**D. Grants Assurance of Salvation**
Romans 8:16; Ephesians 1:13-14

**E. Fills and Overflows**
Acts 2:4, 4:31; Ephesians 5:18

**F. Equips the Believer for Effective Ministry**
Acts 1:8; I Corinthians 12:7-11; also Romans 12:3-8; Matthew 25:15; I Corinthians 4:7; Ephesians 4:11

**G. Produces the Fruit of Character**
Galatians 5:22-23; Philippians 1:11; James 3:17; also Colossians 1:10; Psalms 92:13-14; Matthew 13:23; John 15:2; Romans 5:3-4; II Corinthians 6:6; I Peter 1:5-7

**H.    Enhances Communications with God**
1.    Prayer – Jude 20; Romans 8:26
2.    Worship – Philippians 3:3; John 4:23-24
1.    Spiritual Singing – Ephesians 5:18-20; Colossians 3:16; I Corinthians 14:15

**I.    Guides the Believer in Life**
Romans 8:14; John 16:13; Acts 10:19-20, 13:2

**J.    Quickens the Body at the Resurrection**
Romans 8:11; II Corinthians 3:18

**III.    THE HOLY SPIRIT PREPARES THE BRIDE**
This is another amazing ongoing activity of the Holy Spirit. The Holy Spirit prepares the Bride. In many passages of Scripture non-personal things typify the Holy Spirit. But in this activity, the Holy Spirit is presented in a shadow-type manner as a Person. Let's consider two such examples from Genesis 24 and beyond and the insightful Book of Esther.

**A.    From the Book of Genesis in Life of Isaac and Rebekah – Nine Distinct Works of the Servant**

1.    Genesis 24 - The servant ruled over all of Abraham's possessions and is given stewardship over all the Father's inheritance.
2.    Genesis 24:2-3 – Here the nameless man is given the task of going and leading Isaac, Abraham's son, to his bride.
3.    Genesis 24:10 – He came with ten gift-bearing camels.
4.    Genesis 24:13-21 – Rebekah's response determined her destiny.
5.    Genesis 24:22-30 – Rebekah was set apart by the gifts she accepted from the servant.
6.    Genesis 24:25, 31 – Rebekah and her family provided a dwelling place for the servant and his camels.
7.    Genesis 24:58-59 – The servant became the guide to take her to the bridegroom.
8.    The servant was Rebekah's only source of information about both Isaac and Abraham – the Father and the Son.
9.    The servant's job was finished when he delivered Rebekah to Isaac and he asked nothing for himself.

**B.    From the Book of Esther – Nine Ways Esther Is a Pattern**

1.    Esther had a special responsibility towards the Jewish People in a time of trouble.
2.    Esther had an unpublicized kinship with the Jewish people.
3.    Esther 4:6 – She was ready to lay for life down.

4. Esther was called to a private role of intercession.
5. Her intercession required prayer and fasting.
6. Esther 5:1 – She put on her royal apparel before going into see the King.
7. Esther 5:2 – Her conduct won her the King's favor.
8. She was chosen and entered into royal authority.
9. Esther 6:9 – Esther changed the course of history and saved her entire people by her invention.

So it is with the Bride of Christ and the nature and activity of the Holy Spirit at work in the Last Days. He, the Spirit of Truth, the Guide, the Equipper, has come to prepare the bride for her divine appointment of ruling and reigning with Christ.

As we put together these two beautiful depictions in their poetic pictures, we see a fullness of the ongoing ministry and work of the Holy Spirit. He initiates and we respond. He initiates but we must respond. Will you respond in a personal, relational manner to the Holy Spirit in your life?

## IV. THREE THINGS TO ALWAYS DO WITH THE HOLY SPIRIT

Oh the precious Dove of God! Here are three practical things in our relationship with Him to always do! Remember, this is about having an actual relationship with God!

### A. Honor Him as God – John 16:13

He is more than just a special guest that we temporarily welcome to our house. Don't just invite Him to your home (temple) as though He is going to just come and visit for a short Holiday! No! Honor Him as God! Acknowledge Him as God with His own distinct personality.

### B. Seek Him – Luke 7:7-11

Ask for Him and seek to be equipped by Him. We need His help to live this Christian life successfully. Ask the Father in Jesus name to be empowered with the Holy Spirit. Cry out, "More Lord! Right here, right now!"

### C. Give Him Freedom and Liberty – II Corinthians 3:17

Yield to Him! He is the Spirit of Truth. When the Holy Spirit is Lord, there will be true freedom and liberty. Let Him have absolute control in every area of your life. Then turn around and by the present day activity of the Dove of God, set others free in Jesus' name!

# Reflection Questions
## Lesson Six: Holy Spirit, You Are Welcome Here!

*Answers can be found in the back of the study guide.*

1. Because we want to know the Holy Spirit, it is very significant to know His names that illustrate part of His nature, _____, function, _____, and _____.

2. Symbols are often tools to grant us more understanding about the Holy Spirit. List the six symbols of the Spirit of God:

   a. _____

   b. _____

   c. _____

   d. _____

   e. _____

   f. _____

3. The Holy Spirit is the one who convicts of _____, _____ and the _____ to come.

4. He (the Holy Spirit), the Spirit of Truth, the Guide, the Equipper, has come to prepare the _____ for her divine appointment of ruling and reigning with Christ.

5. What are three things to always do with the Holy Spirit?

    1. _____

    2. _____

    3. _____


6. Review Section II, – "The Holy Spirit's Relationship to the Believer". Choose at least two of the ten works of the Holy Spirit that stand out to you in your own life and then write a short paragraph on your personal experience in that area. Read what you have written as a testimony and allow gratitude to God to fill your heart for what He has done for you.

# Section Two:

# Knowing God by Knowing His Word

# Lesson Seven:
# Knowing the Master Builder

## I. SCRIPTURES ON BUILDING A PROPER FOUNDATION

**F. I Corinthians 3:9-10 – You Are God's Building**

*"For we are God's fellow workers; you are God's field, God's building. According to the grace of God which was given to me, like a wise master builder I laid a foundation, and another is building on it. But each man must be careful how he builds on it."*

**A. Ephesians 2:22 – Built Together for a Habitation of God**

*"In whom you also are being built together into a dwelling of God in the Spirit."*

**B. Colossians 2:6-7 – Firmly Rooted and Built Up in Him**

*"Therefore as you have received Christ Jesus the Lord, so walk in Him, having been firmly rooted and now being built up in Him and established in your faith, just as you were instructed, and overflowing with gratitude."*

**C. Acts 20:32 – Grace Builds Us Up!**

*"And now I commend you to God and to the word of His grace, which is able to build you up and to give you the inheritance among all those who are sanctified."*

**D. Hebrews 5:12-14; 6:1-3 – Let Us Lay Properly the Elementary Principles of Christ**

Hebrews 5:12-14 – *"For though by this time you ought to be teachers, you have need again for someone to teach you the elementary principles of the oracles of God, and you have come to need milk and not solid food. For everyone who partakes only of milk is not accustomed to the word of righteousness, for he is an infant. But solid food is for the mature, who because of practice have their senses trained to discern good and evil."*

Hebrews 6:1-3 – *"Therefore leaving the elementary teaching about the Christ, let us press on to maturity, not laying again a foundation of repentance from dead works and of faith toward God, of instruction about washings and laying on of hands, and the resurrection of the dead and eternal judgment. And this we will do, if God permits."*

**E.    Jude 20 – Build Yourself Up!**

*"But you, beloved, building yourselves up on your most holy faith, praying in the Holy Spirit."*

## II.    THE FOUNDATION IS THE ROCK – CHRIST JESUS

### A.    Old Testament Passages Foretell This Truth

1.    Isaiah 28:16 – A stone for the foundation.
2.    Psalms 18:2 – The Lord is my Rock.
3.    Psalms 62:1-7 – He alone is the Rock of my salvation.

### B.    New Testament Passages Reveal This Truth

1.    I Corinthians 3:11 – Christ Jesus is the foundation.
2.    Acts 4:11-12 – The Stone which the builders rejected...
3.    Ephesians 2:19-21 – Christ the Cornerstone.
4.    I Peter 2:6 – Chief Cornerstone, precious, elect.

## III.    CHRIST JESUS IS THE ROCK OF OUR SALVATION

### A.    Jesus' Own Words Confirm This Truth

1.    Matthew 16:13-18

*"Now when Jesus came into the district of Caesarea Philippi, He was asking His disciples, 'Who do people say that the Son of Man is?' And they said, 'Some say John the Baptist; and others, Elijah; but still others, Jeremiah, or one of the prophets.' He said to them, 'But who do you say that I am?' Simon Peter answered, 'You are the Christ, the Son of the living God.' And Jesus said to him, 'Blessed are you, Simon Barjona, because flesh and blood did not reveal this to you, but My Father who is in heaven. I also say to you that you are Peter, and upon this rock I will build My church; and the gates of Hades will not overpower it.'"*

2.    The Greek word for Peter is *"Petros"* which means small stone or a pebble.

3.   The Greek word for rock is *"petra"* which means large rock.

Jesus is using a "play on words" in His teaching here. He is not identifying Peter as the rock; on the contrary, He is contrasting Peter with Rock! Our lives are not built upon the life and words of a mere man (small stone), but on the Rock (Petra) of Ages which is immovable, unshakable and reliable.

**B.   Four Successive Phases**

There are four successive phases by which each believer takes his place upon this foundation. These are exemplified by the experience of Peter.

1.   A direct, personal confrontation of Peter by Christ. Jesus and Peter stood face to face. There was no middleman. No other human being played any part at all in the experience.

2.   A direct, personal revelation given to Peter. Matthew 16:17 states, "Flesh and blood has not revealed this to you, but my Father who is in heaven." It was not the outcome of natural reasoning or intellectual attainment. It was the direct spiritual revelation to Peter by God the Father Himself!

3.   It demanded a personal acknowledgement by Peter of the truth that had been granted to him.

4.   This was done by an open and public confession by Peter of the truth he acknowledged. (We can each have this same fourfold encounter with Jesus Christ!)

**C.   Three Possible Stages of People**

Where the true Apostolic Gospel of the Kingdom of God is not preached, it results in half-baked believers who might be the "House of Man" not yet truly in the "House of God." Consider these three possible characteristics of mankind in our journey of becoming.

1.   Careless Sinners – those without any manifest concern for salvation.

2.   Awakened Sinners – those under the spirit of conviction but not yet possessing a true saving knowledge with experience of Christ Jesus.

3.   Born Again Believers – those who are supernaturally born of the Spirit by possessing the very life of God within them accompanied by the witness of the Spirit (Romans 8:9, 16).

**D.   What Is Your Experience?**

1.   John 16:13-14 – Revelation given by the Holy Spirit.
2.   Hebrews 13:8 – He remains the same.
3.   John 17:3 – Imparts eternal life.
4.   I John 5:13, 20 – Believe in the Name.
5.   II Timothy 1:12 – I know whom...
6.   Job 22:21 – Acquaint yourself with Him.

## IV.   BUILDING UPON THE FOUNDATION

**A.   Hearing and Doing the Words of Christ**

1.   Matthew 7:24-27
*"Therefore everyone who hears these words of Mine and acts on them, may be compared to a wise man who built his house on the rock. And the rain fell, and the floods came, and the winds blew and slammed against that house; and yet it did not fall, for it had been founded on the rock. Everyone who hears these words of Mine and does not act on them, will be like a foolish man who built his house on the sand. The rain fell, and the floods came, and the winds blew and slammed against that house; and it fell--and great was its fall."*

a)   Notice the difference between the one called "wise" and those called "foolish."
b)   Notice the similarities.
c)   Therefore, build your house solid so as to endure the tests of life (compare to Acts 14:22).

**B.   The Bible – the Written Word, and Christ – the Living Word**

1.   John 1:1 – The Word was God.
2.   John 1:14 – The Word became Flesh.
3.   Revelation 19:13 – His Name is called the Word of God.

### C. Want a Relationship with Jesus? Have a Relationship with His Word!

1.  John 14:19-23

    *"'After a little while the world will no longer see Me, but you will see Me; because I live, you will live also. In that day you will know that I am in My Father, and you in Me, and I in you. He who has My commandments and keeps them is the one who loves Me; and he who loves Me will be loved by My Father, and I will love him and will disclose Myself to him.' Judas (not Iscariot) said to Him, 'Lord, what then has happened that You are going to disclose Yourself to us and not to the world?' Jesus answered and said to him, 'If anyone loves Me, he will keep My word; and My Father will love him, and We will come to him and make Our abode with him.'"*

2.  Proof of Discipleship
    a)  Keeping God's Word is the supreme feature which distinguishes the disciple of Christ.
    b)  Keeping God's Word is the supreme test of the love for God and the supreme case of God's favor toward the believer.
    c)  Christ manifests Himself to the disciple through God's Word, as it is kept and obeyed.
    d)  The Father and the Son come into the life of the disciple and establishes their abiding home with him through God's Word (compare to I John 2:4-5).

### D. The Spirit and the Word Agree!

1.  Acts 2:17 – God speaks through various supernatural means.
2.  I Thessalonians 5:19-21 – All revelation must be tested by the standards of God's Word (compare to Isaiah 8:20; Matthew 24:23-25; I Tim 4:13).
3.  Psalms 33:6 – From creation onward.
    God's Word and God's Spirit work in unity and harmony. They must work the same way in the life of each believer (compare to Genesis 1:2).

# Reflection Questions
## Lesson Seven: Knowing the Master Builder

*Answers can be found in the back of the study guide.*

1. Psalms 11:3 says, *"If the _____ are destroyed, what can the righteous do?*

2. The Old Testament _____ and the New Testament _____ the truth that Christ Jesus is our Rock and our Foundation.

3. When Jesus told Peter, "Upon this rock I will build My church, and the gates of Hades shall not prevail against it" (Matthew 16:18), what was and is the "rock" Jesus was speaking of?

4. What are four successive phases by which each believer takes his or her place upon this foundation, as exemplified in the life of Peter?

    a. _____

    b. _____

    c. _____

    d. _____

5. Review Section III, letter C. Think about the stages and significant events in your "journey of becoming." Which are you right now?

*Continued on the next page.*

6. Review Section III, letter D. Look up each verse. Which verse best describes your present experience with Christ? Explain why.

7. Review Section IV. Ask God to show you what building upon the foundation of Christ might look like for you in the days ahead.

8. In response to what you hear from the Lord, write out one or two "keepable" action steps that you want to implement consistently for the next month (and continue after that). Be as specific as possible.

# Lesson Eight:
# God's Trustworthy Word

## I. THE AUTHORITY OF SCRIPTURE

### A. John 10:34-36 – Titles Used by Christ

*"Jesus answered them, 'Has it not been written in your Law, I said, 'you are gods?' If he called them gods, to whom the Word of God came (and the Scripture cannot be broken), do you say of Him, whom the Father sanctified and sent into the world, 'You are blaspheming,' because I said, 'I am the Son of God'?"*

1. "Your Law"

   In these verses, Jesus quotes from Psalms 82:6 as He speaks to the Jews gathered around him (John 10:27-34) and refers to it as "your Law" (see also John 8:17, 12:34, 15:25; Romans 3:19, I Corinthians 14:21).

2. "Word of God"

   By using this phrase, Jesus indicated that the truths revealed in it do not have their origin with men, but are God inspired. Though God has used many human instruments to compose the Bible, there is authentically only one source – God Himself.

3. "The Scripture"

   The phrase "the Scripture" means literally "that which is written." Therefore, the Bible does not contain the entire knowledge of God. It is the authoritative portion of the Word of God for mankind that is written.

4. "The Scripture Cannot Be Broken"

   This short phrase, "cannot be broken," contains within it every claim for supreme and divine authority that can ever be made on behalf of the Bible. (In actuality, you cannot "break" the 10 Commandments or any portion of the Word of God. If you disobey them, they will break you!)

### B. II Timothy 3:16 – Inspired by the Holy Spirit

All Scripture is inspired by God and profitable for teaching, for reproof, for correction, for training in righteousness.

1. The word translated "by inspiration" means literally "inbreathed of God" and is connected with the word spirit.

2. The Holy Spirit is the invisible, but inerrant, influence who controlled and directed those who made the different books collectively called the Holy Bible.

**C. II Peter 1:20-21 – Moved by the Holy Spirit**
But know this first of all, that no prophecy of Scripture is a matter of one's own interpretation, for no prophecy was ever made by an act of human will, but men moved by the Holy Spirit spoke from God.

1. This passage by Peter confirms these truths through a second apostolic voice, that is, that the source is not human but divine.
2. The Greek word translated "moved by" can also be rendered "directed in their course by" or "borne along by."
3. God controlled the vessels who wrote the scriptures by the interplay of His divine Spirit with the spiritual, emotional, mental, and physical faculties of man

**D. Psalms 12:6 – The Purified Word**
*The words of the LORD are pure words; as silver tried in a furnace on the earth, refined seven times.*

1. The picture from this Old Testament passage is taken from the process of purifying silver in a furnace or oven built of clay.
2. The clay (or earthen) furnace represents the human element. The silver represents the divine message. The fire ensures the absolute purity of the silver (the message). The phrase "seven times" indicates the complete and perfect work of the Holy Spirit.
3. Thus the whole picture presented assures us the divine message of Scripture is due to the perfect work of the Holy Spirit to overrule the frailty of human error.
4. God controlled the vessels who wrote the scriptures by the interplay of His divine Spirit with the spiritual, emotional, mental, and physical faculties of man

## II. THE CONSISTENCY OF SCRIPTURE

**A. From the Voice of the Psalms**
Psalms 119:89 – Settled In Heaven
*Forever, O LORD, Your word is settled in heaven.*

1. David, the prophet, king and Psalmist, emphasizes for us here the Word of God is not the product of time but eternity.

2.  This verse is possibly an encouragement of 3,000 years ahead that not only are all the books of the Bible inspired, but specifically the Book of genesis and the first five books of the Bible called the Pentateuch or Torah.

## B.  From the Testimony of Jesus

1.  Matthew 24:35 – My Words Will Remain.
    *"Heaven and earth will pass away, but My words will not pass away."*
    a)  Jesus clearly declares that even the elements of heaven and earth will pass away, but His very words cannot be destroyed.
    b)  The words of Jesus stand through the test of all time, all satanic attacks, and they remain forever the standard of life.

2.  Matthew 4:1-10 – Jesus Confronts the Devil
    a)  In these passages, Jesus is tempted by Satan in the wilderness. Each of the three times Christ answered each temptation by directly quoting from Old Testament scripture.
    b)  Each time Jesus answers by saying, "It is written..." Each time He quotes from the Book of Deuteronomy.
    c)  Even Satan did not deny the absolute authority of scripture. This shows that the enemies of darkness are under subjection to the Word of God – the scriptures themselves.

3.  Matthew 5:17-18 – From the Sermon on the Mount
    *"Do not think that I came to abolish the Law or the Prophets; I did not come to abolish but to fulfill. For truly I say to you, until heaven and earth pass away, not the smallest letter or stroke shall pass from the Law until all is accomplished."*
    a)  The word "jot" is the smallest letter in the Hebrew alphabet. It is the size of an inverted comma.
    b)  The word "tittle" indicates a little curl which is even smaller than a comma in its shape.
    c)  Thus Christ is saying that the original text of the Hebrew Scriptures is so accurate and authoritative that not even one portion of script can be altered or removed.

4. Matthew 22:31-32 – Answering the Sadducees
*"But regarding the resurrection of the dead, have you not read what was spoken to you by God: `I am the God of Abraham, and the God of Isaac, and the God of Jacob'? He is not the God of the dead but of the living."*

   a) Jesus answers the Sadducees question concerning the resurrection from the dead by quoting from the book of Exodus' account of Moses at the burning bush (Exodus 3:6).

   b) Christ uses the phrase, "spoken to you by God." Once again, Jesus confirms and authenticates the Old Testament as the Word of God. This passage quoted, though fifteen centuries old had not lost any of its vitality, accuracy or authority according to Jesus.

5. Matthew 19:3-9 – Answering the Pharisees
*"And He answered and said, 'Have you not read that He who created them from the beginning made them male and female.'*

   a) When quizzed about divorce by the Pharisees, Jesus answered them by referring to the book of Genesis by using the phrase "in the beginning."

   b) This is a direct reference to the Book of Genesis since this is its Hebrew title.

   c) Thus Christ was consistent in His teaching ministry whether answering man of the devil by referring to scripture as the final authority.

## III. THAT THE SCRIPTURE MAY BE FULFILLED

### A. Jesus' Point of Reference
In the recorded teachings of Jesus, we find a consistent thread where Jesus used the scriptures to point to Himself. This was not out of pride but for the purpose of reinforcing the Hebrew Scriptures and allowing the Holy Spirit to open people's eyes to prophetic fulfillment.

1. Consider Matthew 4:12-17 where it tells of the beginnings of His ministry. It says that He withdrew into Galilee leaving Nazareth and settling in the region of Capernaum (verses 12-13). This becomes a fulfillment of Isaiah 9:1-2 (see verses 14-15) where it states these very locations and Christ's mission – that a "light would shine in the darkness." This occurred so that the scriptures may be fulfilled.

2. Consider Luke 24 where it is recorded of Jesus appearing to two of His disciples after His resurrection on the road to Emmaus: "Then beginning with Moses and with all the prophets, He explained to them the things concerning Himself in all the Scriptures." This verse clearly shows us that Jesus came to fulfill the scriptures. They point to Him! Verse 32 tells the disciples response to this encounter: *"They said to one another, 'Were not our hearts burning within us while He was speaking to us on the road, while He was explaining the Scriptures to us?'"* Should not this be our response as well?

**B. The Old Testament Predicts the Life of the Messiah**

The Bible specifically records that each of the following incidents in the earthly life of Jesus took place in fulfillment of Old Testament Scriptures:

His birth of a virgin; His birth at Bethlehem; His flight into Egypt; His dwelling at Nazareth; His anointing by the Holy Spirit; His ministry in Galilee; His healing of the sick; the rejection of His teaching and His miracles by the Jews; His use of parables; His betrayal by a friend; His being forsaken by His disciples; His being hated without a cause; His being condemned with criminals; His garments being parted and divided by lot; His being offered vinegar for His thirst; His body being pierced without His bones being broken; His burial in a rich man's tomb; His rising from the dead on the third day. [5]

## IV. OUR CONCLUSION

The entire earthly life of Jesus was guided in every aspect by the authority and prophetic influence of God's Word. The Word of God is coherent, complete, and all sufficient. From Genesis to Revelation, it reveals the nature and consequences of sin and the way of deliverance from sin, and its consequences through faith in the Lord Jesus Christ! Let us heed these words, listen, and obey. Through them we will find and receive true, abundant, and eternal life!

# Reflection Questions
## Lesson Eight: God's Trustworthy Word

*Answers can be found in the back of the study guide.*

1. According to the Bible, _____ scripture is inspired by God (II Timothy 3:16).

2. *All prophecy of Scripture was made because men who were moved by the _____ _____ spoke from God* (II Peter 1:20-21).

3. Ask God to search your heart and then honestly reflect, "Do I firmly believe that the Bible is the actual words of God, divinely inspired by the Holy Spirit?" or "Do I have doubts as to the origin of the Bible, its accuracy, and its authority to speak into my life today?" Write down any questions or doubts you have about the authority of the Bible. Be as specific and extensive as possible.

4. Name at least three instances where Jesus validated the Scriptures as authoritative, true, and lasting.

    a. _____

    b. _____

    c. _____

*Continued on the next page.*

5. Why did Jesus consistently use the scriptures to point to Himself?

6. Name as many incidents as you can remember in the earthly life of Jesus that were the fulfillment of the Old Testament scriptures.

7. There is extensive evidence that the Bible is what it says it is: the very words of God. Before moving on further in this study, research any questions or doubts you wrote out in question three. I especially recommend reading applicable sections of *Evidence That Demands a Verdict* by Josh McDowell to confront any issues regarding the authority of the Bible (see the resources section in the back of this manual for more information). For questions surrounding the book of Genesis and its authenticity, I recommend looking at online material and the many resources found at www.answeringenesis.org.

8. Write down satisfactory answers to your questions from Question #3 so you can move forward in faith, able to rely upon the authenticity and reliability of the Word of God.

# Lesson Nine:
# Hungry for His Every Word

## I.   INTRODUCTION – A REVIEW

A study of the Bible must begin with recognition of its divine authority as the Word of God. The Bible is a record of God's word to man, recorded by men who were moved by the Holy Spirit (II Peter 1:21). Since it is the Word of God and not the word of men, its power and authority originate with God Himself. All scripture is inspired by God ("God breathed" – II Timothy 3:16) and so has all the integrity and dependability of God.

Any attempt to understand God and His ways without the Word of God is fruitless. The Bible must be the starting point of all doctrinal discussion, because it is God's revelation of Himself to mankind.

## II.   WHAT COMPRISES THE BIBLE?

The Bible is made up of 66 books, divided into two testaments (i.e., covenants): the Old Testament and the New Testament. It was written down by approximately 44 inspired authors over a period spanning 1,600 years. The Old Testament contains 39 books, spanning the time period from the creation of the world to the return of the Israelites from Babylonian exile. The New Testament contains 27 books, covering the time from Jesus' birth to the end of the 1st century.

### A.   The Old Testament
The 39 books of the Old Testament can be divided into five major parts: Pentateuch, History, Poetry, the Major Prophets, and the Minor Prophets. These books contain the story of God's dealings with His chosen people, the Israelites, and are recognized by Jews today as their canon (the genuine and inspired scriptures, God's Word to the Jewish race).

## The major divisions of the Old Testament are as follows:

The Law (Pentateuch)
Genesis
Exodus
Leviticus
Numbers
Deuteronomy

History
Joshua
Judges
Ruth
I & II Samuel
I & II Kings
I II Chronicles
Ezra
Nehemiah
Esther

Poetry & Wisdom
Job
Psalms
Proverbs
Ecclesiastes
Song of Solomon

Major Prophets
Isaiah
Jeremiah
Lamentations
Ezekiel
Daniel

Minor Prophets
Hosea
Joel
Amos
Obadiah
Jonah
Micah
Nahum
Habakkuk
Zephaniah
Haggai
Zechariah
Malachi

1.  Original Language
    The Old Testament was written down in Hebrew, a Semitic language akin to Arabic. Small segments of Ezra, Daniel, and one verse in Jeremiah, are written in Aramaic (the language of Palestine in Jesus' day).

2.  Archaeological Proofs
    Numerous attempts by critical scholars have failed to prove that facts listed in the Old Testament are erroneous. Here is just one of many examples:

    At least 47 times the Old Testament makes mention of a group of people called the "Hittites." However, in no other ancient writings was there any mention of this nation. Skeptical scholars, during the late 19th century, used to point out this "mythical" kingdom as proof that one couldn't trust the historical facts written in the Old Testament. Then in 1906, a German archaeologist unearthed the ruins of a large city in modern-day Turkey, which proved to be the capital of a vast empire, the Hittite empire. Its existence had up to this time been little known and only suspected by archaeologist, yet the Old Testament had been speaking of Hittites for thousands of years.[6]

Today, archaeological expeditions in the Middle East continue to prove the authenticity of the Old Testament.

3.    How It Was Recorded
Although at first God's revelations were oral (Genesis 15:1), He later commanded that what He had spoken should be written down (Exodus 34:27). Throughout the history of Israel, there were men who recorded what God was doing or saying (Numbers 33:2; Deuteronomy 17:18; Joshua 24:26; I Samuel 10:25; Isaiah 8:16; Jeremiah 36:2).

These writings were the scriptures to the people of God at that time, and God expected them to revere them as such (Joshua 1:8; Psalms 1:2). These books have been passed down to our day and make up what is now known as the Old Testament.

When reading the Old Testament, it is important that one realize that all the books in it look forward. When man fell, God promised a redeemer (Genesis 3:15), and the books of the Old Testament point to that Redeemer. Whether by allusion or direct prophecy, you'll find Jesus in every book of the Old Testament.

The Old Testament is the history of the nation of Israel declaring God's promise that He was going to send a Redeemer to purchase our salvation.

**B.   The New Testament**
The New Testament consists of 27 books written by 8 authors over a 50-year period. It can be roughly divided into five segments: the Gospels, History, the Epistles of Paul, the General Epistles, and Revelation.

The Gospels are a record of the life, death and resurrection of Jesus Christ; the Acts give you a history of the early Church; the Epistles are letters from apostles to churches explaining Christian doctrines; Revelation is John's record of a vision of the end times that he received while in exile on the isle of Patmos.

While the Old Testament contains God' promise of a Redeemer, the New Testament tells us how that Redeemer cam and what He accomplished. The major divisions of the New Testament are as follows:

Gospels
Matthew
Mark
Luke
John

History
Acts

Epistles of Paul
Romans
I & II Corinthians
Galatians
Ephesians
Philippians
Colossians
I & II Thessalonians
I & II Timothy

General Epistles
Titus
Philemon
Hebrews
James
I & II Peter
I, II & III John
Jude

Prophecy
Revelation

1. Original Language
   The New Testament was written in Greek. This includes the gospels even though the language, which Jesus and all the men of Palestine spoke at that time, was Aramaic, not Greek.

   At the time the New Testament was written, Greek was a worldwide language. A gospel written in Aramaic or Hebrew would only be useful in Palestine, but one written in Greek could be read anywhere in the known world. Thus, the Greek language was an invaluable tool in the early spreading of the gospel.

2. How It Was Recorded
   Although the books of the New Testament are arranged somewhat chronologically, they were not written in that order. The first New Testament "scripture" anyone received in those days was oral, coming from the mouths of those who preached the gospel. Paul commended those who received his teaching "not as the word of men," but as the divinely inspired Word of God (I Thessalonians 2:13).

The first part of the New Testament to be written down was the Epistles (specifically, the epistles of Paul). These were written during the period 48-60 A.D. The gospels, written from about 60-100 A.D., were recorded from the inspired memory of those who had walked with Jesus and the inspiration of the Holy Spirit while He was on the earth.

It is generally believed that the entire New Testament was written before the end of the first century A.D.

3.  How It Was Compiled
    It was common practice among the churches in the 1st century to share and exchange letters written by the apostles to the churches. In fact, this practice was encouraged by Paul himself (Colossians 4:16). In this way, each church began to accumulate the various writings of the apostles. Remember, at this time there were no printing presses; these handwritten copies of the gospels and epistles were the only available scripture. One had to come to the place of fellowship to hear the scriptures; this is why Paul exhorted Timothy to practice the "public reading of scripture". (I Timothy 4:13)

    Consider what those early believers had for New Testament scriptures – a handful of laboriously written copies. What a privilege it is for us to have such easy access to the Word of God. Let's not waste that privilege by failing to read what the modern technology has made so conveniently available to us.

## C.  Progressive Revelation

When studying the Old and New Testaments, the following guideline is an aid in rightly dividing the word of truth: Always interpret the Old Testament in the light of the New Testament! The Bible is progressive revelation. The Old Testament foretells the coming of a Messiah; the gospels tell us of His coming; the epistles (especially the epistle of Paul) tell what He accomplished through His death and resurrection.

One cannot fully understand all the things written in the Old Testament without knowledge of the New Testament revelation of Christ. Even the men who wrote the Old Testament under the inspiration of the Holy Spirit didn't fully understand all they had written because Christ had not yet been revealed (I Peter 1:10-11). The Ethiopian eunuch needed someone with a working knowledge of Christ by revelation to explain to him the meaning of Isaiah 53. (Acts 8:30-35)

With the New Testament to shed light on it, the Old Testament becomes all the more a rich treasury of the knowledge of God, full of examples and instruction which are invaluable to a New Covenant believers. (I Corinthians 10:11)

## III. THE GOAL: READ YOUR BIBLE TILL IT READS YOU!

### A. II Timothy 2:15 – Study to Show Yourself Approved

*Be diligent to present yourself approved to God as a workman who does not need to be ashamed, accurately handling the word of truth.*

1. Every believer needs to know the Word of God FULLY. To be our best and to use our faith effectively, we must continually take in the Word of God. Many believers find it difficult to study the Word, and some seem to have little or no interest. The need to give all diligence to the study of the Word was never greater than in our time.

2. The Word of God alone holds the answer for abundant life for present-day believers. Paul's command in II Timothy 2:15 is still our guiding light in these days of spiritual darkness. As we follow Paul's direction and study the Word, our light will grow brighter and brighter. Don't just study the epistles – become a letter send by God for others to read!

### B. Why Should We Study the Bible?

1. Jesus said we should, "Search the scriptures..." (John 5:39). Those who did search the scriptures daily were more noble than the others (Acts 17:11).

2. Solomon, the wisest man of his day, said, *"My son, attend to my words; incline your ear unto my sayings. Let them not depart from your eyes; keep them in the midst of your heart. For they are life unto those that find them, and health to all their flesh"* (Proverbs 4:20-22).

3. David set the example and also taught us to study (Psalms 1:1-6).

4. Peter teaches us as newborn babies to desire the milk of the Word, which is to learn the facts of scripture and how these events relate one to another (I Peter 2:2-4). Also in the milk stage, we begin to learn that the Bible has several major themes running throughout its pages. We begin to learn to identify various doctrines that set forth Bible principles and guides for both faith and practice.

5.  Jeremiah teaches us to both find the Word and to eat it as bread (Jeremiah 15:16). Jesus is the bread of life. How hungry are you?

6.  Paul shows us that there is also a level of Bible study for the mature and skillful at interpreting the Word, which is called strong meat. Peter speaks of the strong meat of Paul's writings, as things hard to be understood which the ignorant do twist to their own destruction (Hebrews 5:11-14).

7.  James tells us that studying the Word is like looking into the mirror of liberty where we can see what our rights are in Christ. This is like a lawyer studying his legal rights as set forth under the laws of the land and then applying them daily in his practice (James 1:22-25). Therefore, look daily in the mirror of God's Word.

## IV. HOW CAN WE STUDY THE BIBLE MOST EFFECTIVELY?

### A. II Corinthians 1:13-14 – Study to Understand

For we write nothing else to you than what you read and understand and I hope you will understand until the end; just as you also partially did understand us, that we are your reason to be proud as you also are ours, in the day of our Lord Jesus.

1.  Read the text and context. Read chapter by chapter, day by day (Deuteronomy 17:19). Read that it may be well with you all the days of your life (Isaiah 34:16). No one that reads out of the book shall fall.

2.  Acknowledge Jesus' Lordship when you read. Put yourself in the Word (II Corinthians 2:13). Let His truth and light permeate your darkness. Read the Word of God with conviction that it is God's Word historical and God's Word present tense.

3.  Read prayerfully with the Holy Spirit's help, and take note of those things which stand out. Date them in your Bible.

4.  Mark your Bible with various colors of ink pens, underlining to draw your attention again to those things noted by the Spirit – for these verses are building blocks for future development of knowledge and truth.

5.  Study themes such as Redemption and ask: (1) How? (2) When? (3) Where? (4) Why?

6. Study the life of important people in the Bible, and then ask yourself and consider:

    a) Why did God choose them?
    b) What did they do to comply with God's dealing?
    c) Consider the processes God used in bringing them to His purposes.
    d) Seek for lessons from their lives that will help you learn faith and patience (Hebrews 6:12; Romans 15:4).

7. Use a study Bible and concordance and follow cross-references, listing the many ways each word is used. Many times you will find several opening to greater truth. Cross-references will help keep you from a narrow viewpoint.

8. Use a concordance and research the original word usage, for often the meaning is clearer than in the English.

9. Use a lexicon and study both the etymology of the word, other ways it has been translated, and where it appears in scripture.

10. Always be ready to enlarge your knowledge and viewpoint as more truth becomes clear.

*"For we know in part... But when that which is perfect is come, then that which is in part shall be done away"*
(I Corinthians 13:9-10).

Knowledge and doctrine come to us little by little, line upon line. *"Whom shall he teach knowledge and whom shall he make to understand doctrine? Them that are weaned from the milk, and drawn from the breasts. For precept must be upon precept, precept upon precept, line upon line: here a little, and there a little."* (Isaiah 28:9-10).

The Book of Acts tells us of Apollos and says, *"He began to speak boldly in the synagogue; but when Priscilla and Aquila heard him, they took him and expounded to him the way of God more accurately"* (Acts 18:24-28).

As we learn the Word and ways of God more perfectly, we are changed and enlarged into His image. *"But we all, with open face beholding as in a glass the glory of the Lord, are changed into the same image from glory to glory, even as by the Spirit of the Lord."* (II Corinthians 3:18).

**B. Joshua 1:8 – Meditate on the Word**

*"This book of the law shall not depart out of your mouth, but you shall meditate on it day and night, that you may be careful to do according to all that is written in it; for then you shall make your way prosperous, and then you shall have good success."*

1.  The word "meditate" means to mutter to oneself, to muse, to ponder, to reflect. In effect, it is repeating the Word to ourselves over and over again. Meditation will unlock the scriptures to your spirit and enable the Holy Spirit to reveal to you the things of God (I Corinthians 2:11-12). (See the lesson, "Christian Meditative Prayer" in my *Consecrated Contemplative Prayer Study Guide* for more details.)

2.  As we meditate in the Word and allow the Word to *"dwell in us richly"* (Colossians 3:16), the Holy Spirit will begin to show us the reality of the spiritual realm which the Word describes (I Corinthians 2:9-10).

**C. Summary – Give the Word First Place**

God Himself has exalted His Word above even His own Name. (Psalms 138:2). As His children we also need to exalt the Word and make it the priority in our lives. By putting the Word first in your life, you'll experience far more of God's life and blessing. The Word shadows clearly who God is and what He has done in us and for us. God's Word is full of His life and power, and if we'll meditate on it, plant it in our hearts, and mix it with active faith, we'll begin to experience that life and power in fuller and fuller measure. Give the written Word and the living Word first place in your life!

# Reflection Questions
## Lesson Nine: Hungry for His Every Word

*Answers can be found in the back of the study guide.*

1. Write out two enlightening insights into the Old Testament from Section II (or something that freshly impacted you).

2. Write out two enlightening insights into the New Testament from Section II (or something that freshly impacted you).

3. II Timothy 2:15 says that God wants us to handle the word of truth

   _____.

4. What does it mean to meditate on the Word? Describe what that might look like for you practically?

*Continued on the next page.*

5.  Review Section IV, A – "Study to Understand". Choose at least two of the ten ways and write them below. Incorporate them immediately into your study habits and with the goals you wrote down in the exercise in Lesson 1. Ask the Lord to help you give the written Word and the Living Word (Christ Himself) first place in your life.

6.  Evaluate your own interest and habits in studying God's Word for yourself. List below any hindrances that are keeping you from pursuing the consistent study of the Bible. Be as specific as possible, and then ask God for His strategy (write it down) and strength to overcome these obstacles so you can "read your Bible until it reads you."

# Lesson Ten:
# The Uniqueness of God's Word

## I. THE NATURE OF GOD'S WORD

### A. Hebrews 4:12 – God's Word Is Alive, Active and Effective

*"For the word of God is living and active and sharper than any two-edged sword, and piercing as far as the division of soul and spirit, of both joints and marrow, and able to judge the thoughts and intentions of the heart."*

Compare the following verses:
1. John 6:63 – The Words of Jesus Are Life
2. II Thessalonians 2:15 – Stand Firm on the Word

### B. James 1:21 – The Condition of the Heart Needed to Respond Properly

*"Therefore, putting aside all filthiness and all that remains of wickedness, in humility receive the word implanted, which is able to save your souls."*

Compare the Following Verses:
1. Romans 9:20 – Potter & The Clay
2. Job 40:2 – God Has No Faults
3. Psalms 25:8-9, 12-14 – The Great Instructor

### C. I Corinthians 1:18 – Different Reactions to the Message of the Cross

*"For the word of the cross is foolishness to those who are perishing, but to us who are being saved it is the power of God."*

Compare the Following Verses:
1. Matthew 10:34 – The Dividing Sword
2. Revelation 1:16 – The Sword of His Mouth

## II. FIRST EFFECT AND BENEFITS OF GOD'S WORD: FAITH

### A. Romans 10:17 – Three Successive Phases

*"So faith comes from hearing, and hearing by the Word of Christ."*

1. First – God's Word Must Be Released
2. Second – God's Word Penetrates Man and Is Heard
3. Third – Hearing then Results in Faith

**B.   I Chronicles 17:23 – Let It Be as the Lord Has Spoken**

*"Now, O LORD, let the word that You have spoken concerning Your servant and concerning his house be established forever, and do as You have spoken."*

**C.   Luke 1:38 – Scriptural Faith**

It begins to be produced within the soul of man by hearing the Word of God. But it must be followed by a step of action (declaration of the mouth or other appropriate response) that expresses this belief. This causes the "word of faith" not to just remain "within man" but activates into the eternal realm where spiritual activity results.

*"And Mary said, 'Behold, the bond slave of the Lord; may it be done to me according to your word.'"*

**D.   Hebrews 11:6 – Faith Pleases God!**

*"And without faith it is impossible to please Him, for he who comes to God must believe that He is and that He is a rewarder of those who seek Him. Faith is the first and indispensable requirement in those who come to God."*

1.   You must believe in the goodness of God!
2.   God is a rewarder of those who diligently seek Him.

## III.   SECOND EFFECT OF GOD'S WORD: THE NEW BIRTH

**A.   James 1:18 – The Results of the Word of Truth**

*"In the exercise of His will He brought us forth by the word of truth, so that we would be a kind of first fruits among His creatures."*

1.   The Christian possesses a new kind of spiritual life within him by God.
2.   This is a result of the Word of Truth being declared, heard, received and then acted upon.
3.   We are His first fruits!

**B.   I Peter 1:23 – An Incorruptible Life Is Ours!**

*"For you have been born again not of seed which is perishable but imperishable, that is, through the living and enduring word of God."*

1.   We are born again through the seed of God's Word.
2.   This seed is not perishable – it never dies out!
3.   Let us live and abide in this Word.

**C.**    **I John 3:9 – An Overcoming Life Results**
*"No one who is born of God practices sin, because His seed abides in him; and he cannot sin, because he is born of God."*

  1.   When the living seed of God's Word abides in us, we will not remain in a constant state of sin.

  2.   This is not referring to "perfection", but that conviction comes upon the believer who abides in God's Word and then confession of sin results.

  3.   Let us make sure and continue to plant God's Word in our soul, so that we will live an overcoming life.

**D.**    **Ephesians 4:22-24 – The Contrast of the Old and New Man**
*"That, in reference to your former manner of life, you lay aside the old self, which is being corrupted in accordance with the lusts of deceit."*

  1.   We must die to "self" – that is to put off the old man or fleshly nature.

  2.   We must renew ourselves by the Spirit in our soul – mind, will and emotions.

  3.   This new man is created in the likeness Christ Jesus in righteousness, holiness and truth.

## IV.   THIRD EFFECT: SPIRITUAL NOURISHMENT

**A.**    **I Peter 2:1-2 – Long for the Pure Milk of God's Word**
*"Therefore, putting aside all malice and all deceit and hypocrisy and envy and all slander, like newborn babies, long for the pure milk of the word, so that by it you may grow in respect to salvation."*

  1.   Put away five things: a) malice, b) guile, c) hypocrisy, d) envy, and e) slander.

  2.   Like newborn babes, love the milk of God's Word.

  3.   As you feed upon the pure milk, you will grow in your spiritual condition.

**B.**    **Matthew 4:4 – Eat the Bread of God**
*But He answered and said, "It is written, 'Man shall not live on bread alone, but on every word that proceeds out of the mouth of God.'"*

  1.   Man then grows into another dimension of his development – where he is no longer satisfied with milk alone, but lives by the bread of God's Word. Bread is a part of everyone's daily diet!

2.   It is the ever-proceeding word that has come, comes again, and keeps on coming that satisfies the soul of man. This again implies an on-going living relationship with both the written and the living Word of God.

### C.   Hebrews 5:12-14 – Chew on the Strong Meat of God's Word

*"For though by this time you ought to be teachers, you have need again for someone to teach you the elementary principles of the oracles of God, and you have come to need milk and not solid food. For everyone who partakes only of milk is not accustomed to the word of righteousness, for he is an infant. But solid food is for the mature, which because of practice have their senses trained to discern good and evil."*

1.   Maintain what you attained. Keep a devotional life of reading the Word of God. But do not stop there.
2.   Press on to maturity and chew on and digest the strong meat of God's Word by being a hearer and a doer of it.
3.   Jesus said, *"My meat is to do the will of Him who sent me."*
4.   What meat are you chewing on?

## V.   FOURTH EFFECT: PHYSICAL HEALING AND HEALTH

### A.   Psalms 107:17-20 – Healing and Deliverance Are Ours

*"Fools, because of their rebellious way, And because of their iniquities, were afflicted. Their soul abhorred all kinds of food, and they drew near to the gates of death. Then they cried out to the LORD in their trouble; He saved them out of their distresses. He sent His word and healed them, and delivered them from their destructions."*

Note: God sent His Word and healed them. How can you partner with God in the sending and receiving His Word so that healing may come?

### B.   Isaiah 55:11 – God's Will Accomplishes Its Intended Purposes

*"So will My word be which goes forth from My mouth; It will not return to Me empty, Without accomplishing what I desire, And without succeeding in the matter for which I sent it."*

Note: Our confidence rests in God's very nature. What He states, He will back! God's desire is that His Word succeeds.

**C.  Proverbs 4:20-22 – Our Complete Provision**

*"My son, give attention to my words; Incline your ear to my sayings. Do not let them depart from your sight; Keep them in the midst of your heart for they are life to those who find them and health to all their body."*

Four Directions on God's Medicine Bottle:
1.  Attend to My words.
2.  Incline your ear.
3.  Let them not depart from your eyes.
4.  Keep them in the midst of your heart.

**D.  Matthew 15:26-28 – Healing Is the Children's Bread**

*"And He answered and said, 'It is not good to take the children's bread and throw it to the dogs. But she said, 'Yes, Lord; but even the dogs feed on the crumbs which fall from their masters' table.' Then Jesus said to her, 'O woman, your faith is great; it shall be done for you as you wish.' And her daughter was healed at once."*

1.  If the dogs get to eat the crumbs from His table, then what does He feed Kings and Priests who are invited to feast at His table of delights?
2.  Jesus interpreted this desperate woman's statements as statements of authentic faith.

**E.  Psalms 78:41 – Do Not Limit God**

*"Again and again they tempted God, and pained the Holy One of Israel."*

Note: Do not let religious traditions of men, teachings of unbelief, and false cessationism doctrines rob you of God's riches made available through the Word of God.

1.  Compare with the teachings of Matthew 15:6-9.
2.  Compare with the passage in Isaiah 29:13.

**F.  Psalms 34:8 – Taste the Medicine of God's Word for Yourself!**

*"O, taste and see that the LORD is good. How blessed is the man who takes refuge in Him!"*

Yes, taste the goodness of the Lord. His will is good. His Word is good. The Lord is good indeed!

# Reflection Questions
## Lesson Ten: The Uniqueness of God's Word

*Answers can be found in the back of the study guide.*

1. According to Hebrews 4:12, the Word of God is _____,
   _____, and _____, and able to
   _____.

2. According to James 1:21, the Word of God is _____
   to some, but the _____ _____ _____ to others.

3. What are four effects of God's Word?

   a. _____   c. _____

   b. _____   d. _____

4. It is impossible to please God without _____.

5. I Peter 1:23 says that we are born again of seed that is _____,
   through the _____ and _____ Word of God.

6. What are three stages of spiritual nourishment?

   a. _____

   b. _____

   c. _____

*Continued on the next page.*

7.  When God's Word goes out, it _____ all that He desires and _____ in the matter for which He sent it (Isaiah 55:11).


8.  Which effect are you most desiring. Why? Ask God to accomplish His Word for you in this area.

# Lesson Eleven:
# The Effects of God's Word

I. **REVIEW ON THE FIRST FOUR EFFECTS OF GOD'S WORD**

   A. **Faith**

   B. **The New Birth**

   C. **Spiritual Nourishment**

   D. **Physical Healing and Health**

II. **THE FIFTH EFFECT: ILLUMINATION AND UNDERSTANDING**

   A. **Psalms 119:130**
   *"The unfolding of Your words gives light; It gives understanding to the simple."*

     1. The entrance of God's Word produces understanding and mental illumination.
     2. It cannot be replaced by natural education or intelligence.

   B. **Hebrews 4:12 – God's Word Permeates the Whole Man**
   *"For the word of God is living and active and sharper than any two-edged sword, and piercing as far as the division of soul and spirit, of both joints and marrow, and able to judge the thoughts and intentions of the heart."*

III. **THE SIXTH EFFECT: VICTORY OVER SIN AND SATAN**

   A. **Psalms 119:11**
   *"Your word I have treasured in my heart, that I may not sin against You."*

     1. David stored up God's Word in his heart.
     2. Therefore it was always available for immediate use in every time of need.

   B. **Psalms 17:4 – We Can Be Free from Satan's Deceptive Ways**
   *"As for the deeds of men, by the word of Your lips I have kept from the paths of the violent."*

**C.** **I Corinthians 10:31 and Colossians 3:17 – Two Universal Standards of Conduct:**

    1.    All to the glory of God.
    2.    All in the Name of Jesus.

**D.** **I Corinthians 3:16-17; 6:19-20**

    1.    The Christian's body is the temple of the Holy Spirit.
    2.    Compare with I Thessalonians 4:3-4.
    3.    Guided by these standards Christians can be preserved from the harmful effects of sin and Satan.

**E.** **Ephesians 6:17 – God's Word Is the Spirit's Sword**
*"And take the helmet of salvation, and the sword of the Spirit, which is the Word of God."*

**F.** **Luke 4:1-13 – Jesus Used God's Word to Conquer Satan**
*"Jesus, full of the Holy Spirit, returned from the Jordan and was led around by the Spirit in the wilderness for forty days, being tempted by the devil. And He ate nothing during those days, and when they had ended, He became hungry.*

*"And the devil said to Him, 'If You are the Son of God, tell this stone to become bread.' And Jesus answered him, 'It is written, "Man shall not live by bread alone."'*

*"And he led Him up and showed Him all the kingdoms of the world in a moment of time. And the devil said to Him, 'I will give You all this domain and its glory; for it has been handed over to me, and I give it to whomever I wish. Therefore if You worship before me, it shall all be Yours.' Jesus answered him, 'It is written, "You shall worship the Lord your God and serve Him only."'*

*"And he led Him to Jerusalem and had Him stand on the pinnacle of the temple, and said to Him, 'If You are the Son of God, throw Yourself down from here; for it is written, "He will command his angels concerning you to guard you," and "On their hands they will bear you up, so that you will not strike your foot against a stone."' And Jesus answered and said to him, 'It is said, "You shall not put the Lord your God to the test."'*

*"When the devil had finished every temptation, he left Him until an opportune time."*

**G.   I John 2:14 – Young Believers Overcome by Abiding in the Word**
Ecclesiastes 11:10 states that there is no distinction between old and young, male and female.

**H.   Colossians 2:8 – Philosophy and Secular Education**
Compare I Timothy 6:20 – Nothing can displace the priority of God's Word.

**I.   Revelation 12:11 – Victory over Satan**
*And they overcame him because of the blood of the Lamb and because of the word of their testimony, and they did not love their life even when faced with death.*

1.   By the Blood of Jesus
2.   By the Word of God
3.   By the Word of Our Testimony

**J.   Hosea 4-6 – Ignorance Brings Destruction**
*"My people are destroyed for lack of knowledge. Because you have rejected knowledge, I also will reject you from being My priest. Since you have forgotten the law of your God, I also will forget your children."*

## IV.   REVIEW ON EFFECTS FIVE AND SIX OF GOD'S WORD

**A.   Illumination and Understanding**

**B.   Victory over Sin and Satan**

## V.   THE SEVENTH EFFECT: CLEANSING AND SANCTIFICATION

**A.   Ephesians 5:25-27**
*"Husbands, love your wives, just as Christ also loved the church and gave Himself up for her, so that He might sanctify her, having cleansed her by the washing of water with the word, that He might present to Himself the church in all her glory, having no spot or wrinkle or any such thing; but that she would be holy and blameless."*

Compare with John 15:3.

**B.   I John 1:7; 5:6 – The Purpose for Christ Coming**

1.   As savior to redeem by His blood
2.   As teacher to sanctify by His Word.

C. **Exodus 30:17-21 – The Tabernacle of Moses**

*"The Lord spoke to Moses saying, 'You shall also make a laver of bronze, with its base of bronze, for washing; and you shall put it between the tent of meeting and the altar, and you shall put water in it. Aaron and his sons shall wash their hands and their feet from it; when they enter the tent of meeting, they shall wash with water, so that they will not die; or when they approach the altar to minister, by offering up in smoke a fire sacrifice to the Lord. So they shall wash their hands and their feet, so that they will not die; and it shall be a perpetual statute for them, for Aaron and his descendants throughout their generations.'"*

D. **Hebrews 10:12 – Holiness Is God's Eternal Nature**

The Process of Sanctification
1. Romans 12:1-2
2. Romans 8:29

E. **II Peter 1:2-4 – Sanctification Is Included in God's Provision**

*"Grace and peace be multiplied to you in the knowledge of God and of Jesus our Lord; seeing that His divine power has granted to us everything pertaining to life and godliness, through the true knowledge of Him who called us by His own glory and excellence. For by these He has granted to us His precious and magnificent promises, so that by them you may become partakers of the divine nature, having escaped the corruption that is in the world by lust."*

## VI. THE EIGHTH EFFECT: OUR MIRROR OF SPIRITUAL REVELATION

A. **James 1:23-25**

*"For if anyone is a hearer of the word and not a doer, he is like a man who looks at his natural face in a mirror; for once he has looked at himself and gone away, he has immediately forgotten what kind of person he was. But one who looks intently at the perfect law, the law of liberty, and abides by it, not having become a forgetful hearer but an effectual doer, this man will be blessed in what he does.'*

B. **II Corinthians 5:17-18, 21 – The New Creation in Christ**

*"Therefore if anyone is in Christ, he is a new creature; the old things passed away; behold, new things have come. Now all these things are from God, who reconciled us to Himself through Christ and gave us the ministry of reconciliation.... He made Him who knew no sin to be sin on our behalf, so that we might become the righteousness of God in Him."*

**C.**   **Song of Songs 4:7 – The Beauty of Christ's Bride**
*"You are altogether beautiful, my darling, and there is no blemish in you."*

**D.**   **II Corinthians 3:18 – Transformed by the Mirror of God's Word**
*"But we all, with unveiled face, beholding as in a mirror the glory of the Lord, are being transformed into the same image from glory to glory, just as from the Lord, the Spirit."*

**E.**   **II Corinthians 4:17-18 – Afflictions Release Glory**
*"For momentary, light affliction is producing for us an eternal weight of glory far beyond all comparison, while we look not at the things which are seen, but at the things which are not seen; for the things which are seen are temporal, but the things which are not seen are eternal."*

## VII. THE NINTH EFFECT: OUR JUDGE

**A.**   **Genesis 18:25**
*"Far be it from You to do such a thing, to slay the righteous with the wicked, so that the righteous and the wicked are treated alike. Far be it from You! Shall not the Judge of all the earth deal justly?"*

Compare with the following scriptures:
1.   Judges 11:27
2.   Psalms 58:11
3.   Isaiah 33:22

**B.**   **John 3:17 – God Delights in Mercy**
*"For God did not send the Son into the world to judge the world, but that the world might be saved through Him."*

**C.**   **I Peter 1:17 – The Office of Judgment**
*"If you address as Father the One who impartially judges according to each one's work, conduct yourselves in fear during the time of your stay on earth...."*

Compare with John 5:22-23 and John 5:26 –27.

**D.**   **John 12:47-48 – Final Authority Is God's Word**
*"If anyone hears My sayings and does not keep them, I do not judge him; for I did not come to judge the world, but to save the world. He who rejects Me and does not receive My sayings has one who judges him; the word I spoke is what will judge him at the last day."*

119

Compare with the following scriptures:
1.  Isaiah 66:2
2.  Matthew 5:18
3.  Matthew 24:35

**E.  Revelation 2:11-13 – The Last Great Judgment**
*"He who has an ear, let him hear what the Spirit says to the churches. He who overcomes will not be hurt by the second death. And to the angel of the church in Pergamum write: The One who has the sharp two-edged sword says this: 'I know where you dwell, where Satan's throne is; and you hold fast My name, and did not deny My faith even in the days of Antipas, My witness, My faithful one, who was killed among you, where Satan dwells.'"*

**F.  I Corinthians 11:31 – Delivered from God's Judgment**
*"But if we judged ourselves rightly, we would not be judged."*

# Reflection Questions
## Lesson Eleven: Discovering The Effects of God's Word

*Answers can be found in the back of the study guide.*

1. Another effect of the Word of God is that it brings _____
   and _____.

2. According to Psalms 119:11, David's strategy to overcome sin was to
   _____ God's words in his heart. What does this mean
   for you? Describe what it might look like in your life each day.

3. Revelation 12:11 says that *we will overcome by the* _____
   _____ _____ _____ *and the* _____
   _____ _____.

4. I Peter 1:2-4 says that *"His divine power has granted to us everything*
   *pertaining to* _____ *and* _____, *through the*
   *true knowledge of Him who called us by His own glory and excellence. For by*
   *these He has granted to us His precious and magnificent promises, so that by*
   *them you may become partakers of the* _____
   _____, *having escaped the corruption that is in the world*
   *by lust."*

5. In the verses above, was Peter referring only to our lives once we get to
   heaven, or to what God has provided for us now on earth?

   _____

*Continued on the next page.*

6. Name an area in your life where you would like God's Word to bring light and give understanding. Write that area down and ask God to reveal His Word to you, and look for Him to answer your prayer in the coming days.

7. Review Romans 12:1-2. What steps do you see Paul laid out as a process for sanctification? Write them out below. Ask the Lord to speak to you about the process of sanctification in your own life. Personalize what God says to you from Romans 12:1-2 and take action accordingly.

# Lesson Twelve:
# Getting to Know God

## I.   BEHOLDING THE BEAUTY OF THE LORD

As we round the bend on our journey of discovering the heart of God and His Word, I sense the intense desire of the Holy Spirit to take a whiskbroom and dust off some of The Lost Treasures of the Body of Christ and present them as brilliant gems to gaze upon. Like a spiritual archaeologist or perhaps something like a modern day "Indiana Jones" of the fabled movies, let's search thru the treasure chest of God and church history and bring these jewels to the forefront once again.

So pull up a chair right alongside me as we eat the last serving in this full course meal at the banquet table of His amazing grace and lavish love. He wants us to not only grow in our knowledge of Him, He wants us to Know Him in a transforming manner. Remember, the more I know Him the more I love Him.

One of the "Lost Arts" being recovered in growing more intimate with our Lord and gazing upon His beauty is the time-tested model called Christian Meditative Prayer. So let's start there for now and build upon these understandings.

### A.   Toward a Working Definition

   1.   Elmer L. Towns – Vice President of Liberty University
       a)   "Christian Meditation is not about what methods you use, nor is it about what position you assume, nor is it about what you chant or how you focus. Christian Meditation is about God, it is meditation that will change your life because you focus on God – and when you experience God, it is God who changes you." [7]

   2.   Peter Toon – Author of *Meditating as a Christian*
       a)   "Meditation is...thinking about, reflecting upon, considering, taking to heart, reading slowly and carefully, prayerfully taking in, and humbly receiving into mind, heart and will that which God has revealed. For Christian meditating...is being guided and inspired by the indwelling Spirit of Christ in the consideration of God's revelation." [8]

3.    Dietrich Bonhoeffer – German Author of *The Way of Freedom*
      a)    "Just as you do not analyze the assets of someone you love, but accept them as they are said to you, then accept the word of Scripture and ponder it in your heart, as Mary did. That is all. That is meditation." [9]

4.    Dr. Sam Storms – Author and Founder of Enjoying God Ministries
      a)    "Meditation, then, is being attentive to God. It is a conscious, continuous engagement of the mind with God. This renewing of the mind (Romans 12:1-2) is part of the process by which the Word of God penetrates the soul and spirit with the light of illumination and the power of transformation." [10]

5.    Tricia McCary Rhodes – Author of *The Soul at Rest*
      a)    "The Bible is not a rulebook, a history lesson, or a treatise to be dissected and analyzed. We come to its author with our hearts open and our desire for Him....Seeking God's face, we want to understand the person who wrote these powerful words. Our hearts are the soil in which the word is planted. Every part of our being joins together to nourish the seeds of truth until they sprout and bring life to our soul." [11]

6.    Dr. Siang-Yang Tan – Author of *Disciplines of the Holy Spirit*
      a)    "Meditation is pondering over scripture verses or passages in such a way that the written Word of God becomes a living word of God applied to our hearts by the Holy Spirit. The two primary words for meditation in the Bible mean 'to murmur or mutter' and 'to speak to oneself.' Meditation is a process of thinking through language that takes place in the heart or inner life. The truth being meditated upon moves from the mouth (murmuring), to the mind (reflective thinking), and finally to the heart (outer action). The person meditating seeks to understand how to relate Bible truth to life." [12]

## B.    Some Analogies to Help Our Understanding

1.    Richard J. Foster – Author of *Prayer: Finding the Heart's True Home*
      a)    "Have you ever watched a cow chew its cud? This unassuming animal will fill its stomach with grass and other food. Then it settles down quietly and, through a process of regurgitation, reworks what it has received, slowly moving its mouth in the process. In this way it is

able to fully assimilate what it has previously consumed, which is then transformed into rich, creamy milk. So it is with meditative prayer. The truth being mediated upon passes from the mouth into the mind and down into the heart, where through quiet rumination – regurgitation, if you will – it produces in the person praying, a loving, faith-filled response." [13]

2. Donald S. Whitney – Author of *Spiritual Disciplines for the Christian Life*
   a) "A simple analogy would be a cup of tea. You are the cup of hot water and the intake of Scripture is represented by the tea bag. Hearing God's Word is like one dip of the tea bag into the cup. Some of the tea's flavor is absorbed by the water, but not as much as would occur with a more thorough soaking of the bag. In this analogy, reading, studying, and memorizing God's Word are represented by additional plunges of the tea bag into the cup. The more frequently the tea enters the water, the more effect it has. Meditation, however, is like immersing the bag completely and letting it steep until all of the rich tea flavor has been extracted and the hot water is thoroughly tinctured reddish brown." [14]

3. Dr. Siang-Yang Tan – *Disciplines of the Holy Spirit*
   a) "In meditation, we seek to enter into the Scripture and live in it. We stand in the shoes of the disciples, alongside the Pharisees, in the kitchen with Martha, at the feet of Jesus with Mary. As St. Ignatius encourages us to do, we let all of our senses come into play. We see the friends lowering the paralytic through the roof. We smell the salt sea, feel the cool breeze on our face, and hear the lapping of waves along the shore of Galilee. We taste the bread multiplied by Jesus' hands as we sit among the crowd. As the Spirit works, we take time to meet Jesus in each passage, to have lunch with Him, to address Him and to be addressed by Him, to touch the hem of His garment." [15]

## II.  SEVEN PRACTICAL GUIDELINES

### A.  Seven Guidelines for Meditating on God's Word

The following seven guidelines all begin with the letter "P".

1.  Prepare
    a)  Always begin by practicing the presence of the living God. Perhaps reading and chewing on Psalms 139:1-10 will help. Focus your attention on God's inescapable presence, the intimate nearness of God Himself. Remember, we want to encounter the living Word of God.

    b)  Issues of *posture, time,* and *place* are really secondary, but not unimportant. The only rule would be: *do whatever is most conducive to receiving.* If a posture is uncomfortable, change it. If a particular time of day or night is inconvenient, change it. If the place you have chosen exposes you to repeated interruptions and distractions, move it. Now select your scripture text.

2.  Peruse
    a)  By this I mean, read, repeat the reading, write it out, re-write it, etc. Read your verse(s) aloud ever so slowly and marinate in their beauty.

    b)  We must keep in mind the difference between *informative* reading of the Scriptures and *formative* reading. The former focuses on the collecting information, the increase of knowledge, and memorization of data. The purpose of the latter is to **be formed** or **shaped** by the Word by the ministry of the Holy Spirit. With informative reading, I am in control of the text. With formative reading, the text controls me.

    c)  Concerning formative reading, Peter Toon writes:
        (1)  "I do not hold the Bible in my hand in order to analyze, dissect or gather information from it. Rather I hold it in order to let my Master penetrate the depths of my being with his Word and thus facilitate inner moral and spiritual transformation. I am there in utter dependence upon our God – who is the Father to whom I pray, the son through whom I pray, and the Holy Spirit in whom I pray." [16]

3.  Picture
    a)  Next apply your sanctified imagination and your surrendered natural senses to the truth contained within the scripture verse. Then personally engage in a relationship with the Holy Spirit to encounter or experience what the text speaks. Hear, feel, taste, smell, and see the truths God reveals.

    b)  Sanctify your thoughts and desires by the blood of Jesus. Then in worship to the One True God, Jesus Christ the Lord, let the Holy Spirit fill your senses—your entire being. This then can be a useful tool by which we experience more intimately and powerfully the reality of who God truly is.

4.  Ponder
    a)  Reflect on the truth of the Word; brood over the truth of the chosen scripture; absorb it, soak in it, as you turn it over within your heart and soul. By all means, internalize and personalize the passage. Let the Word speak to you!

5.  Pray
    a)  This is now one of my favorite parts of the process. Take the truths, which the Holy Spirit has illuminated, and now pray it back to God, whether in petition, thanksgiving, or intercession, spiritual warfare, declaration or even some form of poetic reflection. I often sing my scripture based prayers back to God. It adds oil to the entire dynamic.

6.  Praise
    a)  Worship the Lord for who He is and what He has done and how it has been revealed in Scripture. Offer thanksgiving and the sacrifice of praise. Meditation ought always to lead us into adoration and celebration of the Personhood of God Himself.

7.  Practice
    a)  Commit yourself to doing what the Word commands. The aim of Christian meditative prayer is moral transformation. The goal is "Incarnational Christianity." The ultimate aim of Biblical contemplation is obedience. (See Joshua 1:8; Psalms 119:11.)

### B. Keeping It Simple

1. Remember.
2. Think on these things.
3. Ponder deeply.
4. Behold the rich love of God.
5. Muse on the works of His hands.
6. Meditate.
7. Consider.
8. Let the mind of Christ be in you.
9. Set your mind on things above.
10. Let the Word of Christ dwell in you richly.

## III. BENEFITS OF CHRISTIAN MEDITATIVE PRAYER

### A. The Benefits of Scriptural Meditation [17]

1. You gain insight and instruction of truth (Psalms 119:99 – II Timothy 2:7).
2. You get a positive outlook on life (Psalms 104:34).
3. You deepen your love for the Scriptures and God (Psalms 119:97).
4. You become prosperous as you apply the insights gained (Joshua 1:8).
5. You grow and become stable in the Christian life (Psalms 1:2-3; John 15:4).
6. You develop a strong prayer life (John 15:7).
7. You are motivated to ministry (I Samuel 12:24; I Timothy 4:15).
8. You are motivated to repent and live better (Psalms 39:3; Revelation 2:5).
9. You find the peace of God (Philippians 4:8-9).
10. You get a clear focus to guide you in making decisions (Matthew 6:33 – Colossians 3:2).
11. You focus your life on Christ (Hebrews 12:3; I John 3:1).
12. You worship God in His majestic Glory (Deuteronomy 4:39).

### B. The Blessings of Christian Meditation

1. Divine Protection: Psalms 91:1
2. Heart's Desire: Psalms 37:4
3. Joy of the Lord: Psalms 104:34
4. Peace of God: Isaiah 26:3
5. Overcoming Anger: Psalms 4:4
6. Overcoming Fear: Deuteronomy 7:17-19
7. Overcoming Sin: Psalms 119:11

8. Renewed Mind: Romans 12:2
9. Stability: Psalms 37:31
10. Wisdom: Psalms 49:3

## IV. THE GOAL: GETTING TO KNOW THE NEARNESS OF GOD

### A. Getting Comfortable with God

Many of us struggle with resting and waiting in God's presence, perhaps because we think He has something against us or we are just too busy. While He calls us into change, He does so by wrapping His arms of love all around us. God delights in hug therapy.

This might take some time before you learn to trust that the best place to be is in your Father's arms. But this will happen. Why? Because He is more committed to the journey than you are! So come on in and commune with Him. Encounter Him. He is waiting for you.

### B. A Poem of Reflection about the Present Tense God

*I Am* **by Helen Mallicoat** (Public Domain)

I was regretting the past
and fearing the future.

Suddenly, my Lord was speaking.
"My name is I Am."

He paused. I waited. He continued.

"When you live in the past,
with its mistakes and regrets,
it is hard. I am not there.
My name is not "I was"

When you live in the future,
with its problems and fears,
It is hard. I am not there.
My name is not "I will be"

When you live in this moment,
It is not hard. I am here.
My name is "I AM."

**C.    Glimpses of Eternity from Hebrews 12:22-24**

*"But you have come to Mount Zion and to the city of the living God, the heavenly Jerusalem, and to myriads of angels, to the general assembly of the firstborn who are enrolled in heaven, and to God, the Judge of all, and to the spirits of the righteous made perfect, and to Jesus, the mediator of a new covenant, and to the sprinkled blood, which speaks better than the blood of Abel."*

Yes, I look forward to eternity worshipping God 24/7/365 with the countless number of angels and the all heavenly hosts and with the likes of Abraham and Sarah, Moses and Aaron, Esther, Daniel, Isaiah, Mary of Bethany, Peter and Paul, Phoebe and John the beloved. I can't hardly wait till I on the other side, when I get in the heavenly reception line to give thanks to Andrew Murray, Saint Theresa of Avila, Watchman Nee, Charles Spurgeon, Corrie ten Boom, A.W. Tozer, D.L. Moody, Aimee Simple McPherson, Derek Prince, Bob Jones and so many other heroes and heroines of the faith.

I can only imagine what that day will be like when I am rejoined with my parents, grandparents, my late beloved wife, and so many of my friends that have gone on before me. I can only imagine.

But there is another reality. I don't have to wait to enter into worship and adoration. I get to taste a realm of heaven on earth every day. I have practice sessions everyday on Getting to Know the Heart of God. Oh what a joy set before us!

**D.    Getting to Know You – Getting to Know All About You!**

Well here we are at the close of another lesson, another chapter, another class, another book. "What have you left for the closing, Dr. Goll?" you might be thinking. Oh, I have something special for sure. As many of you know, before I was ever a preacher, an international ambassador or global intercessor, I was first a singer and a worshipper from a small rural town. I tend to always go back to my sweet spot, and so I will once again. Ponder with me a while...

Yes, I have picked the famous show tune from the brilliant musical, *The King and I* by Rodgcrs and Hammerstein! The majestic and romantic portrayal of a relationship between a woman living a far off in some distant land with the children she teaches and the King who earnestly looks upon. The endearing song of this enchanting musical is entitled, *"Getting to Know You"!* (I wish I could quote all the lyrics here, but I can't due to copyright regulations.)

In the many laps within this journey, we have been getting to know "You" – the living Word of God. We have been learning all about

You—drawing closer discovering what it means to allow You to be our dearest Friend.

From now until forever, we can sing of our Passionate Pursuit of getting to know God and becoming intimately familiar with all His amazing attributes. Yes, this is what it is all about. This is what carries over into all time — all eternity.

Getting to Know You!

It really is the subject I like most. And I capitalized the word *You*, of course. Getting to know You—the Living God. Yes, I trust in this time together, I have been able to give you some tools to aid you in your personal quest so that you can get to know a God as Father, Jesus as Messiah and Holy Spirit as your personal tutor and guide, and to gaze upon the amazing nature of God's Word.

This is not just information we need—it is a heart relationship we seek. It is continuing in an abandoned walk with Him, whether our season in life appears to be filled with good days or difficult now. To know Him is to love Him. This is my conclusion after years in the journey—day by day.

**E.   Let This Be Our Prayer**

*"Grace and peace be multiplied to you in the knowledge of God and of Jesus our Lord; seeing that His divine power has granted to us everything pertaining to life and godliness, through the true knowledge of Him who called us by His own glory and excellence. For by these He has granted to us His precious and magnificent promises, so that by them you may become partakers of the divine nature."* (II Peter 1:2-4)

Our Father, in the majestic name of Jesus, I declare that I to know You as intimately as You know me. Draw me nearer, nearer, nearer, precious Lord, to Your ever-loving side. Identify the hard places in my heart and send forth Your Word, which shatters every rock. Give me a greater hunger for the written and living Word of God. By the ministry of the Holy Spirit and Your great grace, and by the power of the shed blood of the Lamb, set me apart and make me wholly Yours. I declare that the chief end of my life is to glorify You and enjoy You forever! Amen and Amen!

# Reflection Questions
## Lesson Twelve: Getting to Know God

*Answers can be found in the back of the study guide.*

1. One of the "Lost Arts" being recovered in growing more intimate with our Lord and gazing upon His beauty, is the model called _____ _____ _____.

2. According to Dr. Sam Storms, "Meditation is a _____, _____ engagement of the mind with God.

3. List the seven guidelines for meditating on God's Word:

    a. _____          e. _____

    b. _____          f. _____

    c. _____          g. _____

    d. _____

4. Psalms 91:1 is an example of divine _____ which is just one among many of the blessings of Christian Meditation.

5. Many of us struggle with _____ and _____ in God's presence, because we think He has something against us or we are just too busy.

6.  Drawing closer to God is to discover what it means to allow Him to be our

_____   _____.

7.  Spend some time pondering the amazing reality that the Living God invites us to know God as Father, Jesus as Messiah and the Holy Spirit as your personal tutor and guide. Ask Him to reveal Himself to you so that you will not only stand in awe of who He is, but also in order that your love for Him would grow to maturity. Write down anything that is revealed to you during this time of reflection.

# Answers to the Reflection Questions

**Lesson One: Getting to Know God and His Word**
1. past, personal/approachable, encountered
2. Name, nature
3. the Father
4. love, blessing
5. human vessels

**Lesson Two: The Amazing Attributes of God**
1. eternal power, divine nature, clearly
2. all powerful, everywhere at the same time, all knowing
3. unity, plurality
4. Sin, Satan, religion

**Lesson Three: Jesus the Messiah Has Come**
1. Who do you say that Jesus is?
2. Messiah; Savior
3. Messiah; Judaism; darkness
4. 129
5. See any of the bold headers in Sections II through V.

**Lesson Four: Wonderful Messiah, Son of God**
1. 130
2. 60, 70
3. No one would have been able to predict the manner of the Messiah's death except by inspiration of the Holy Spirit. The Father knew exactly how His Son would die and foretold/foreshadowed this truth through the Old Testament Scriptures.
4. See any of the bold headers in Sections I and II.

**Lesson Five: The Person of the Holy Spirit**
1. personal conversion, growth in Christ, God's Kingdom
2. co-equal, co-eternal, co-existent
3. the incarnation of Jesus; the earthly ministry of Jesus, the atonement of Jesus, the resurrection of Jesus, the gift of the Holy Spirit
4. to complete the ministry of Christ, to form the corporate Body of Christ, the prepare the Bride of Christ
5. Church, believer
6. always, only

**Lesson Six: Holy Spirit, You Are Welcome Here!**
1. characteristics, purpose, ministry
2. fire, wind, water, a seal, oil, dove
3. sin, righteousness, judgment
4. bride
5. honor Him as God, seek Him, give Him freedom and liberty

**Lesson Seven: Knowing the Master Builder**
1. foundations
2. foretells, reveals
3. The revelation that Jesus was the Christ and the foundation – the Rock – of our faith
4. Direct, personal confrontation; Direct, personal revelation; Personal acknowledgement; Open and public confession

**Lesson Eight: God's Trustworthy Word**
1.    all
2.    Holy Spirit
4.    See Matthew 24:35; Jesus confronts the devil in the wilderness (Matthew 4:1-10); The Sermon on the Mount (Matthew 5:17-18); Answering the Sadducees concerning the resurrection from the dead (Matthew 22:31-32); Answering the Pharisees when quizzed about divorce (Matthew 19:3-9).
5.    For the purpose of reinforcing the Hebrew scriptures and allowing the Holy Spirit to open people's eyes to prophetic fulfillment.
6.    Some include the following: Jesus' birth of a virgin; His birth at Bethlehem; His flight into Egypt; His dwelling at Nazareth; His anointing by the Holy Spirit; His ministry in Galilee; His healing of the sick; the rejection of His teaching and His miracles by the Jews; His use of parables; His betrayal by a friend; His being forsaken by His disciples; His being hated without a cause; His being condemned with criminals; His garments being parted and divided by lot; His being offered vinegar for His thirst; His body being pierced without His bones being broken; His burial in a rich man's tomb; His rising from the dead on the third day.

**Lesson Nine: Hungry for His Every Word**
3.    accurately
4.    To mutter to oneself, to muse, to ponder, to reflect. It is saying the Word to ourselves over and over again. Allowing the Word to "dwell in us richly" (Colossians 3:16) and allowing the Holy Spirit to show us the reality of the spiritual realm which the Word describes (I Corinthians 2:9-10).

**Lesson Ten: The Uniqueness of God's Word**
1.    living, active; sharp, judge the thoughts and intentions of the heart.
2.    foolishness, power of God
3.    faith; the new birth, spiritual nourishment, physical healing and health
4.    faith
5.    imperishable, living, enduring
6.    Pure milk of God's Word, Bread of God, Meat of God
7.    accomplishes, succeeds

**Lesson Eleven: The Effects of God's Word**
1.    illumination, understanding
2.    treasure
3.    blood of the Lamb, word of our testimony
4.    life; godliness; divine nature
5.    What God has provided for us right now on earth.

**Lesson Twelve: Getting to Know God**
1.    Christian Meditative Prayer
2.    conscious, continuous
3.    prepare, peruse, picture, ponder, pray, praise, practice
4.    protection
5.    resting, waiting
6.    dearest, Friend

# Resource Materials

James Montgomery Boice, *Foundations of the Christian Faith*, Downers Grove, IL: IVP Academic Publishers, 1986.

Kevin Conner, *The Foundations of Christian Doctrine*, Portland, OR: City Bible Publishing, 1980.

Andrew Murray, *The Sprinkling of the Blood, and the Trinity*, http://www.webrevival.net/en/books/murray/sprinkling_of_blood.html

James W. Goll, *A Radical Faith*, Book and Study Guide, Ada, MI: Chosen Books, 2011.

Josh McDowell, *The New Evidence That Demands a Verdict*, Nashville, TN: Thomas Nelson; Rev Upd edition, 1999.

Derek Prince, *The Spirit-Filled Believer's Handbook*, Lake Mary, FL: Creation House, 1993.

Merrill F. Unger, *Unger's Bible Dictionary*, Chicago, IL: Moody Press, 1966.

# End Notes

1   Andrew Murray, *The Sprinkling of the Blood, and the Trinity,*

2   Kevin Conner, *The Foundations of Christian Doctrine,* Portland, OR: City Bible Publishing, 1980.

3   James Montgomery Boice, *Foundations of the Christian Faith,* Downers Grove, IL: IVP Academic Publishers, 1986.

4   Dick Iverson, *The Holy Spirit Today,* Portland, OR: Bible Temple Publishing, p. 5.

5   Derek Prince, *The Spirit-Filled Believer's Handbook,* Lake Mary, FL, Creation House, 1993, p. 46.

6   Merrill F. Unger, *Unger's Bible Dictionary,* Chicago, IL: Moody Press, 1966.

7   Elmer L. Towns, *Biblical Meditation for Spiritual Breakthrough,* Ventura, CA: Regal Books, 1999, p. 21.

8   Peter Toon, *Meditating as a Christian: Waiting Upon God,* New York: HarperCollins, 1991.

9   Dietrich Bonhoeffer, *The Way of Freedom,* Harper & Row, 1966.

10  Sam Storms, *Devotional Life Class Notes* (7 Guides to Meditating), Grace Training Center, Kansas City, MO.

11  Tricia McCary Rhodes, *The Soul at Rest,* Minneapolis MN: Bethany House Publishers, 1996.

12  Dr. Siang-Yang Tan and Dr. Douglas H. Gregg, *Disciplines of the Holy Spirit: How to Connect to the Spirit's Power and Presence,* Grand Rapids, MI: Zondervan, 1997.

13  Richard J. Foster, *Prayer: Finding the Heart's True Home,* HarperOne, 1992.

14  Donald S. Whitney, *Spiritual Disciplines for the Christian Life,* Colorado Springs, CO: NavPress, 1991.

15  Tan and Gregg, *Disciplines.*

16  Toon, *Meditating.*

17  Towns, *Biblical Meditation.*

# About the Author

James W. Goll is a lover of Jesus who co-founded Encounters Network (based in Franklin, Tennessee), which is dedicated to changing lives and impacting nations by releasing God's presence through prophetic, intercessory and compassion ministry. James is the International Director of Prayer Storm, a 24/7/365 prayer media-based ministry. He is also the Founder of the God Encounters Training e-School of the Heart – where faith and life meet.

After pastoring in the Midwest, James was thrust into the role of itinerant teaching and training around the globe. He has traveled extensively to every continent, carrying a passion for Jesus wherever he goes. James desires to see the Body of Christ become the house of prayer for all nations and be empowered by the Holy Spirit to spread the Good News around the world. He is the author of numerous books and training manuals as well as a contributing writer for several periodicals.

He is a member of the Harvest International Ministry Apostolic Team and a consultant to several national and international ministries. James and Michal Ann Goll were married for more than 32 years before her graduation to heaven in the fall of 2008. They have four wonderful adult married children and multiple grandchildren, and James continues to make his home in greater Nashville, Tennessee.

# Other Books by James W. and Michal Ann Goll

*God Encounters*

*Prayer Storm*

*Intercession: The Power and Passion to Shape History*

*A Radical Faith*

*Women on the Frontlines Series*

*The Lost Art of Intercession*

*The Lost Art of Practicing His Presence*

*The Lost Art of Pure Worship*

*The Coming Israel Awakening*

*The Beginner's Guide to Hearing God*

*The Lifestyle of a Prophet*

*The Call of the Elijah Revolution*

*The Prophetic Intercessor*

*The Seer Expanded*

*Shifting Shadows of Supernatural Experiences*

*Empowered Prayer*

*Empowered Women*

*Dream Language*

*Angelic Encounters*

*Adventures in the Prophetic*

*Praying for Israel's Destiny*

*Living a Supernatural Life*

*Deliverance from Darkness*

*Exploring Your Dreams and Visions*

*God's Supernatural Power in You*

*The Reformer's Pledge*

*Prayer Changes Things*

*Passionate Pursuit: Getting to Know God and His Word*

*In addition there are numerous study guides including Discovering the Seer in You, Exploring the Gift and Nature of Dreams, Prayer Storm, A Radical Faith, Deliverance from Darkness, Prophetic Foundations, Walking in the Supernatural Life, Consecrated Contemplative Prayer and many others with corresponding CD and MP3 albums and DVD messages.*

## For More Information:

James W. Goll
Encounters Network
P.O. Box 1653
Franklin, TN 37065
Visit: www.EncountersNetwork.com
www.PrayerStorm.com
www.GETeSchool.com
www.CompassionActs.com

Email: info@encountersnetwork.com
Speaking Invitations: InviteJames@encountersnetwork.com

# EN Resources

P.O. Box 1653 | Franklin, TN 37065-1653
www.encountersnetwork.com | 1.877.200.1604

# COMPASSION ACTS
### love taking action

## Love Taking Action

### ◆ Mission Projects
sending resources and volunteers to help meet specific needs

### ◆ Rice Shipments
shipping fortified rice to fight hunger around the world

### ◆ Emergency Relief
responding to natural disasters through food and humanitarian aid

### ◆ Project Dreamers Park
building playgrounds and community centers to inspire children to dream

### ◆ First Nations in America
serving Native Americans by providing food, health supplies and education

**Compassion Acts** is a network of synergistic relationships between people, ministries and organizations, focused on bringing hope for our day through the power of compassion and prayer. We desire to demonstrate love and encourage the hearts of those impacted by poverty, disease, political strife and natural disasters through human relief efforts.

www.compassionacts.com

---

# PrayerStorm

## The Hour that Changes the World

### Leviticus 6:13
*"Fire must be kept burning on the altar continually; it must not got out."*

## Worldwide 24/7
## Hourly Intercession Targeting:

### ◆ Revival in the Church
### ◆ Prayer for Israel
### ◆ World's Greatest Youth Awakening
### ◆ Crisis Intervention through Intercession

The vision of PrayerStorm is to restore and release the Moravian model of the watch of the Lord into churches, homes and prayer rooms around the world. Web-based teaching, prayer bulletins and resources are utilized to facilitate round-the-clock worship and prayer to win for the Lamb the rewards of His suffering.

*Releasing the Global Moravian Lampstand*

www.prayerstorm.com

---

# Encounters Network
### changing lives ❖ impacting nations

## Changing Lives ❖ Impacting Nations

### ◆ Empowering Believers
through training and resources

### ◆ EN Media
relevant messages for our day

### ◆ God Encounters Training
e-school of the heart

### ◆ EN Alliance
a coalition of leaders

The vision of Encounters Network is to unite and mobilize the body of Christ by teaching and imparting the power of intercession and prophetic ministry, while cultivating God's heart for Israel. We accomplish this through networking with leaders in the church and marketplace; equipping believers through conferences and classes, utilizing various forms of relevant media; and creating quality materials to reproduce life in the Spirit.

www.encountersnetwork.com

# GET eSchool Courses & Corresponding Study Guides

## CHAMBER OF ACTION
### EXPLORING PRINCIPLES - EXPERIENCING POWER

### DELIVERANCE FROM DARKNESS

You shall know the truth and the truth shall set you free! Through this accessible and easy-to-use guide, you will learn how to: recognize demonic entities and their strategies, equip yourself to overcome the demonic, keep yourself refreshed during the fight, bring healing through blessing, and much more!

### THE HEALING ANOINTING

In this thorough study guide, James W. Goll covers a range of topics including: The Healing Ministry of Jesus, How to Move In and Cooperate with the Anointing, Healing the Wounded Spirit, Overcoming Rejection, the Five Stage Healing Model, and much more.

### REVIVAL BREAKTHROUGH

James W. Goll brings 12 solid teachings on topics like: Prophetic Prayers for Revival, Classic Characteristics of Revival, Fasting Releases God's Presence, Creating an Opening, Gatekeepers of His Presence, and much more. This manual will inspire you to believe for a breakthrough in your life, neighborhood, region, city and nation for Jesus' sake!

### WAR IN THE HEAVENLIES

These carefully prepared 12 detailed lessons on spiritual warfare cover topics like: The Fall of Lucifer, Dealing with Territorial Spirits, The Weapons of Our Warfare, High Praises, The Blood Sprinkled Seven Times, and other great messages. This is one of James' most thorough and complete manuals.

### RELEASING SPIRITUAL GIFTS

In this study guide, James draws from scripture and adds perspective from many diverse streams to bring you clear definitions and exhort you into activation and release. The topics covered are subjects like: How Does the Holy Spirit Move, What Offends the Holy Spirit, and many other lessons from years of experience.

## CHAMBER OF LIFE
### BUILDING OUR FOUNDATION - KNOWING TRUTHS, GROWING IN FAITH

### A RADICAL FAITH

Whether you are a veteran spiritual warrior or new believer, this accessible, comprehensive guide lays out the enduring biblical fundamentals that establish the bedrock of belief for every mature Christian. This handbook will help you build an indestructible foundation of radical faith.

### WALKING IN THE SUPERNATURAL LIFE

James W. Goll weds together a depth of the Word with a flow of the Spirit that will ground and challenge you to live in the fullness for which God has created you. Topics include The God Who Never Changes, Tools for the Tool Belt, Finishing Well, and much more.

### GETTING TO KNOW GOD AND HIS WORD

These lessons focus on knowing God personally and what He has revealed about Himself in His Word. Lessons include: Knowing the Master Builder, God's Trustworthy Word, The Effects of God's Word, God as Our Personal Father, The Amazing Attributes of God, Jesus the Messiah Has Come, The Person of the Holy Spirit, and more.

TO PURCHASE THESE STUDY GUIDES INDIVIDUALLY
& OTHER RELATED PRODUCT VISIT: WWW.ENCOUNTERSNETWORK.COM

## For Course Information and Registration Visit
## www.GETeSchool.com

# GET eSchool Courses & Corresponding Study Guides

## CHAMBER OF INTIMACY
### BLUEPRINTS FOR PRAYER - PRELUDE TO REVIVAL

### WATCHMEN ON THE WALLS

This original study guide is a classic in today's global prayer movement and covers many important and foundational lessons on intercession including: Fire on the Altar, Christ Our Priestly Model, The Watch of the Lord, From Prayer to His Presence, Identification in Intercession, and more.

### COMPASSIONATE PROPHETIC INTERCESSION

These 12 lessons feature James W. Goll's finest teaching on the fundamentals of prophetic intercession and represent one of the primary messages of his life. Topics include Travail, Tears in the Bottle, Prophetic Intercession, The Power of Proclamation, Praying in the Spirit, and much more.

### PRAYER STORM

This study guide sounds a worldwide call to consistent, persistent prayer for: revival in the church, the greatest youth awakening ever, Israel – and for all the descendents of Abraham, and God's intervention in times of major crises. Prayer Storm is an invitation into an international virtual house of prayer full of intercessors who commit to pray one hour per week.

### PRAYERS OF THE NEW TESTAMENT

In this study guide, James goes through each of the scriptural prayers of the early church apostles and brings you a brief historical background sketch along with insights from the Holy Spirit for today. Learn what true apostolic intercession is, how to intercede with revelation, and how to cultivate a heart for your city and nation.

### PRAYERS THAT STRIKE THE MARK

In these 12 lessons, James W. Goll deals with issues like Confessing Generational Sins, Reminding God of His Word, Praying from a Victorious Perspective, and The Many Faces of Prayer. It is a thorough and precise exposure to the many different strategies and models we can all use in prayer.

### CONSECRATED CONTEMPLATIVE PRAYER

These 12 lessons have helped hundreds come into a deeper communion with their heavenly Father. James W. Goll brings understanding from the truths of Christian mystics of the past and builds on it with lessons from his own walk with the Lord. Topics include The Ministry of Fasting, Contemplative Prayer, Quieting Our Souls before God, and much more.

TO PURCHASE THESE STUDY GUIDES INDIVIDUALLY & OTHER RELATED PRODUCT VISIT: WWW.ENCOUNTERSNETWORK.COM

For Course Information and Registration Visit
# www.GETeSchool.com

Made in the USA
San Bernardino, CA
01 February 2017